lace & eyelet stitches

lace & eyelet stitches

250 to knit

edited by Erika Knight

COLLINS & BROWN

C&B
CRAFTS

First published in the United Kingdom in 2007 by
Collins & Brown
10 Southcombe Street
London
W14 0RA

An imprint of Anova Books Company Ltd

Commissioning Editor: Michelle Lo
Design Manager: Gemma Wilson
Designer: Sarah Rock
Photographer: Michael Wicks
Illustrator: Lotte Oldfield
Assistant Editor: Katie Hudson
Senior Production Controller: Morna McPherson

ISBN 978-1-84340-423-1

A CIP catalogue for this book is available from the British Library.

9 8 7 6 5 4 3 2 1

Reproduction by Dot Gradations Ltd
Printed and bound by SNP Leefung Printers Ltd, China

This book can be ordered direct from the publisher.
Contact the marketing department, but try your bookshop first.

www.anovabooks.com

contents

inspiration

Lace and eyelets create rewarding results and can be configured into patterns and constructed into all kinds of fabrics. Intricacy is the inspiration for this book.

From simple eyelets to gossamer-like cobwebs, lace and eyelet stitches are intriguing and absorbing and offer endless possibilities for experimentation. For the beginner knitter, lace knitting may seem daunting as it often requires a little more technique – wrapping the yarn around the needle a few times, dropping a stitch or two, or (intentionally) slipping un-knitted stitches over a knitted one, for example. However, the sheer sense of accomplishing a simple eyelet will encourage you to attempt and experiment with even prettier effects.

Lace and eyelet stitches are often worked in finer-weight yarns to show off their delicate detailing, yet when the same stitch is worked in a heavy-weight yarn, the holes take on a whole new dimension, prompting one to consider its function beyond a little cardigan or shawl. Lace stitches in robust, rustic tweed yarns are great for home accents, adding texture and a bit of a twist to cushions for, for example, a couch or floor.

Conversely, open-work lace patterns worked in whisper-fine mohair are perfect for delicate shrugs, cardigans or even throws. I love to use two or three different lace or eyelet stitches within one garment. Although this can involve a little mathematics, by working out stitch repeats and experimenting with swatches to ensure each is suitable for the yarn selected, you can ultimately work patterns together into intricate and fascinating designs. Why not create with the swatches themselves? Combining them with printed fabrics creates pretty afghans and cushions for easy glamour.

Eyelets are a constant source of inspiration, easy to create and beautiful in their simplicity. They're often worked in formal, evenly spaced patterns, but consider creating a random design. Scatter them along one side of the top of a cardigan and accent it with threaded ribbon; after all, simple eyelet designs make a perfect canvas for weaving in ribbon, I-cord, or strips of fabric.

In addition, beads worked with either knitted lace or eyelet layouts create a lively embellished textile, especially suitable for small gift projects such as delicate cushions or cardigans. Worked on top of the knitting, they can make a simple and pretty design in themselves and add both practical and decorative detail to your garments.

Some lace patterns may prove to be quite mathematical, providing a challenge and requiring times of concentration, but persevere. The actual process of creating these stitches can be both stimulating and relaxing in itself; keeping count of the many repeats and shaping the fabric is a wooly exercise for the creative brain!

From a technical standpoint, each of these stitches has been tried and tested to ensure accuracy. We've included some old favorites and provided a few new ones, as well. If you're new to knitting, the section devoted to basic skills will ease the process. The key is to continue at it: through trial and error you will discover the endless design possibilities at your fingertips. Knitting is not just a hobby, it can also be a lifestyle.

Whether you choose to challenge yourself or keep it simple, the result is just as rewarding – all kinds of interesting, creative and fabulous fabrics. Experiment, take risks, and let your creativity guide you to discover the amazing effects that can be created with lace and eyelets.

lace knitting

The most stunning patterns can be created with lace. Discover how simple wraps and yarnovers create arresting results.

Lace knitting can be used in many different ways – as an allover pattern, a horizontal or vertical panel, single or random motifs. Lace stitch patterns are most effective when worked in plain yarns, as fluffy or textured yarns do not show the detail of the pattern. Finer yarns are also more suitable than bulky yarns, as they give the stitch a more delicate appearance. Lace knitting is especially popular for baby garments.

Lace patterns are produced by using the eyelet method of increasing. These are usually worked in conjunction with decreases, so that the number of stitches remains constant at the end of each row. However, some of the most beautiful lace effects are achieved by increasing stitches on one or more rows and decreasing the extra stitches on subsequent rows. Circular shawls are produced by continually increasing stitches on every round (or every alternate round), while working the increases into the lace pattern.

Construction of Lace Patterns

The eyelet method of increasing are used in lace patterns to form a hole. The exact way that the yarn is taken over the needle depends on the stitches at either side of the eyelet – whether they are knitted, purled or a combination of both. They are then accompanied by one of the decrease methods, depending on whether the slant is to be towards the left or the right.

tools & equipment

To master any skill, it's imperative to have a solid foundation of the techniques. This section provides useful information that can come in handy while knitting.

Knitting Needles

Knitting needles are used in pairs to produce a flat, knitted fabric. They are pointed at one end to form the stitches and have a knob at the other to retain the stitches. They may be made in plastic, wood, steel, or alloy and range in size from 2mm to 17mm in diameter. In England, needles used to be sized by numbers – the higher the number, the smaller the needle. In America, the opposite is true – higher numbers indicate larger sizes. Metric sizing has now been internationally adopted. Needles are also made in different lengths that will comfortably hold the stitches required for each project.

It is useful to have a range of sizes so that tension swatches can be knitted up and compared. Discard any needles that become bent. Points should be fairly sharp; as blunt needles reduce the speed and ease of working.

Circular and double-pointed needles are used to produce a tubular fabric or flat rounds. Many traditional fisherman's sweaters are knitted in the round. Double-pointed needles are sold in sets of four or five. Circular needles consist of two needles joined by a flexible length of plastic. The plastic varies in length. Use the shorter lengths for knitting sleeves, neckbands, and so on, and the longer lengths for larger pieces such as sweaters and skirts.

Cable needles are short needles that used to hold the stitches of a cable to the back or front of the main body of knitting.

Other Useful Equipment

Needle gauges are punched with holes corresponding to the needle sizes and are marked with both the old numerical sizing and the metric sizing, so you can easily check the size of any needle.

Stitch holders resemble large safety pins and are used to hold stitches while they are not being worked – for example, around a neckline when the neckband stitches will be picked up and worked after back and front have been joined. As an alternative, thread a blunt-pointed sewing needle with a generous length of contrast-colored yarn, thread it through the stitches to be held while they are still on the needle, then slip the stitches off the needle and knot both ends of the contrast yarn to secure the stitches.

Wool sewing needles or tapestry needles are used to sew completed pieces of knitting together. They are large, with a broad eye for easy threading and a blunt point that will slip between the knitted stitches without splitting and fraying the yarn. Do not use sharp-pointed sewing needles to sew up knitting.

A row counter is a cylinder with a numbered dial used to count the number of rows that have been knitted. Push it onto the needle and turn the dial at the end of each row.

A tape measure is essential for checking tension swatches and for measuring the length and width of completed knitting. For an accurate result, always smooth the knitting (without stretching) on a firm flat surface before measuring it.

A crochet hook is useful for picking up dropped stitches.

Knitting Yarn

Yarn is the term used for strands of spun fibre that are twisted together into a continuous length of the required thickness. Yarn can be of animal origin (wool, angora, mohair, silk, alpaca), vegetable origin (cotton, linen), or man-made (nylon, acrylic, rayon). Knitting yarn may be made up from a combination of different fibres.

Each single strand of yarn is known as a ply. A number of plys are twisted together to form the yarn. The texture and characteristics of the yarn may be varied by the combination of fibres and by the way in which the yarn is spun. Wool and other natural fibres are often combined with man-made fibres to make a yarn that is more economical and hard-wearing. Wool can also be treated to make it machine washable. The twist of the yarn is firm and smooth and knits up into a hard-wearing fabric. Loosely twisted yarn has a softer finish when knitted.

Buying Yarn

Yarn is most commonly sold wound into balls of specific weight measured into grams or ounces. Some yarn, particularly very thick yarn, is also sold in a coiled hank or skein that must be wound into a ball before you can begin knitting.

Yarn manufacturers (called spinners) wrap each ball with a paper band on which is printed a lot of necessary information. The ball band states the weight of the yarn and its composition. It will give instructions for the washing and ironing and will state the ideal range of needle sizes to be used with the yarn. The ball band also carries the shade number and dye lot number. It is important that you use yarn of the same dye lot for an entire project. Different dye lots vary subtly in shading; this may not be apparent when you are holding the two balls, but it will show as a variation in shade on the finished piece of knitting.

Always keep the ball band as a reference. The best way is to pin it to the tension swatch (see page 19) and keep them together with any leftover yarn and spare buttons or other trimmings. That way, you can always check the washing instructions and also have materials for repairs.

the basics

Once you have mastered the basics of knitting, you can go on to develop your skills and start making more challenging projects.

Casting On

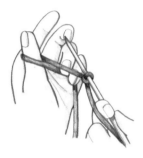

1 Make a slip knot 1m (39in) from the end of the yarn. Hold the needle in your right hand, with the ball end of the yarn over your index finger. Wind the loose end of the yarn around your left thumb from front to back.

2 Insert the point of the needle under the first strand of yarn on your thumb.

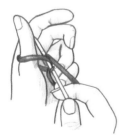

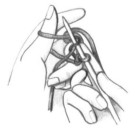

3 With your right index finger, take the ball end of the yarn over the point of the needle.

4 Pull a loop through to form the first stitch. Remove your left thumb from the yarn. Pull the loose end to secure the stitch. Repeat from * until all stitches have been cast on.

Knit Stitch

1 Hold the needle with the cast-on stitches in your left hand, with the loose yarn at the back of the work. Insert the right-hand needle from left to right through the front of the first stitch on the left-hand needle.

2 Wind the yarn from left to right over the point of the right-hand needle.

3 Draw the yarn through the stitch, thus forming a new stitch on the right-hand needle.

4 Slip the original stitch off the left-hand needle, keeping the new stitch on the right-hand needle.

5 To knit a row, repeat steps 1 to 4 until all the stitches have been transferred from the left-hand needle to the right-hand needle. Turn the work, transferring the needle that holds the stitches to your left hand to work the next row.

Purl Stitch

1 Hold the needle with the stitches in your left hand with the loose yarn at the front of the work. Insert the right-hand needle from right to left into the front of the first stitch on the left-hand needle.

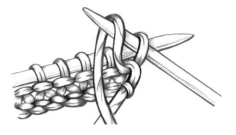

2 Wind the yarn from right to left over the point of the right-hand needle.

3 Draw the yarn through the stitch, thus forming a new stitch on the right-hand needle.

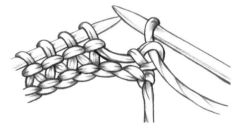

4 Slip the original stitch off the left-hand needle, keeping the new stitch on the right-hand needle.

5 To purl a row, repeat steps 1 to 4 until all the stitches have been transferred from the left-hand needle to the right-hand needle. Turn the work, transferring the needle that holds the stitches to your left hand to work the next row.

Increasing

The simplest method of increasing one stitch is to work into the front and back of the same stitch.

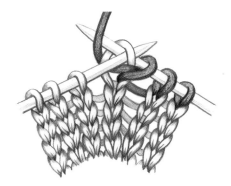

On a knit row, knit into the front of the stitch to be increased; then, before slipping it off the needle, place the right-hand needle behind the left-hand needle and knit again into the back of the same stitch. Slip the original stitch off the left-hand needle.

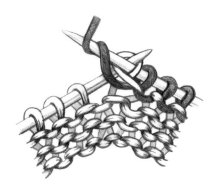

On a purl row, purl into the front of the stitch to be increased into; then, before slipping it off the needle, purl again into the back of the same stitch. Slip the original stitch off the left-hand needle.

Decreasing

The simplest method of decreasing one stitch is to work two stitches together.

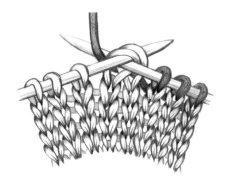

On a knit row, insert the right-hand needle from left to right through two stitches instead of one, then knit them together as one stitch. This is called knit two together (k2tog).

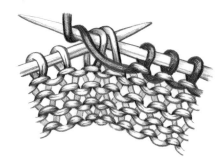

On a purl row, insert the right-hand needle from right to left through two stitches instead of one, then purl them together as one stitch. This is called purl two together (p2tog).

Casting Off

There is one simple, most commonly used method of securing stitches once you have finished a piece of knitting – casting off. The cast-off edge should always have the same 'give' or elasticity as the fabric and you should always cast off in the stitch pattern used for the main fabric, unless the pattern directs otherwise.

Knitwise

Knit two stitches. *Using the point of the left-hand needle, lift the first stitch on the right-hand needle over the second then drop it off the needle. Knit the next stitch and repeat from * until all stitches have been worked off the left-hand needle and only one stitch remains on the right-hand needle. Cut the yarn (leaving enough to sew in the end), thread the end through the stitch, then slip it off the needle. Draw the yarn up firmly to fasten off.

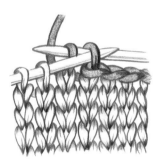

Purlwise

Purl two stitches. *Using the point of the left-hand needle, lift the first stitch on the right-hand needle over the second and drop it off the needle. Purl the next stitch and repeat from * until all the stitches have been worked off the left-hand needle and only one stitch remains on the right-hand

needle. Secure the last stitch as described for casting off knitwise.

The excitement of arriving at the last stage of your knitting can make you castoff without the same care that you have used in the rest of the work. You should take into account the part of the garment you are working on. If it is a neckband, you need to make sure that your cast-off edge is not too tight, preventing the neck from going over the wearer's head. If you are a tight knitter, you may need to cast off with a larger needle. Lace stitches should also be bound off in pattern, slipping, making stitches, or decreasing as you go to make sure that the fabric doesn't widen or gather up.

Tension (gauge)

The correct tension (or gauge) is the most important contribution to the successful knitting of a garment. The information given under this heading at the beginning of all patterns refers to the number of stitches required to fill a particular area; for example, a frequent tension indication would be '22sts and 30 rows = 10cm (4in) square measured over stocking stitch on 4mm needles.' This means that, in order to obtain the correct measurements for the garment you intend to knit, you need to produce fabric made up of the proportion of stitches and rows given in the tension paragraph, regardless of the needles you use. The needle size indicated in the pattern is the one that most knitters will use to achieve this tension, but it is the gauge that is important, not needle size.

The way to ensure that you do achieve the correct tension is to work a tension sample or swatch before starting the main part of the knitting. Although this may seem to be time wasting and a nuisance, it can save the enormous amount of time and aggravation that would result from having knitted a garment the wrong size.

Tension Swatch

The instructions given in the tension paragraph of a knitting pattern are either for working in stocking stitch or in pattern stitch. If they are given in pattern stitch, you need to work a multiple of stitches the same as the multiple required in the pattern. If they are given in stocking stitch, any number can be cast on. Whichever method is used, there should always be enough to give at least 12cm (5in) in width. Work in pattern or stocking stitch according to the wording of the tension paragraph until the piece measures at least 10cm (4in) in depth. Break the yarn about 15cm (6in) from the work and thread this end through the stitches, then remove the knitting needle. Place a pin vertically into the fabric a

few stitches from the side edge. Measure 10cm (4in) carefully and insert a second pin. Count the stitches. If the number of stitches between the pins is less than that specified in the pattern (even by 1cm/½in), your garment will be too large. Use smaller needles and knit another tension sample. If your sample has more stitches over 10cm (4in), the garment will be too small. Change to larger needles. Check the number of rows against the given tension, too.

It is most important to get the width measurement correct before starting to knit. Length measurements can usually be adjusted during the course of the knitting by adjusting the measurements to underarm or sleeve length, which is frequently given as a measurement and not in rows.

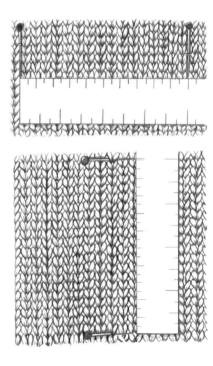

stitch gallery

Slanting Open-Work Stitch

Even number of sts.

1st row (right side): Edge st, *yf, k2tog; rep from * to last st, edge st.

2nd and 4th rows: Purl.

3rd row: K2, * yf, k2tog; rep from * to last 2 sts, k2tog. Rep these 4 rows.

If decreasing in lace-weight yarns proves to be challenging, try using sharp-pointed needles such as Addi Turbos or even bamboo.

Eyelet Rib Variation

Multiple of 8 + 2.

Eyelet openwork is worked on WS rows to clearly indent the rib pattern.

1st row (right side): P2, *k6, p2; rep from * to end.

2nd row (wrong side): K2, *p6, yo, k2tog; rep from * to last 8 sts, p6, k2.

Rep these 2 rows until desired length, end with a RS row.

Next row (wrong side): K2, *p2, yo, k2tog; rep from * to last 4 sts, p2, k2.

Next row (right side): P2, *k2, p2; rep from * to end.

Rep these last 2 rows to cont pat, or work in a variation as desired.

Angel Wings Lace Panel

Worked over 19 sts.

1st row (right side): P2, sl 1, k1, psso, k5, yo, k1, yo, k5, k2tog, p2.

2nd row: K2, p2tog, p5, yo, p1, yo, p5, p2tog tbl, k2.

3rd row: P2, sl 1, k1, psso, k4, yo, k3, yo, k4, k2tog, p2.

4th row: K2, p2tog, p4, yp, p3, yo, p4, p2tog tbl, k2.

5th row: P2, sl 1, k1, psso, k3, yo, k5, yo, k3, k2tog, p2.

6th row: K2, p2tog, p3, yo, p5, yo, p3, p2tog tbl, k2.

7th row: P2, sl 1, k1, psso, k2, yo, k7, yo, k2, k2tog, p2.

8th row: K2, p2tog, p2, yo, p7, yo, p2, p2tog tbl, k2.

9th row: P2, sl 1, k1, psso, k1, yo, k9, yo, k1, k2tog, p2.

10th row: K2, p2tog, p1, yo, p0, yo, p1, p2tog tbl, k2.

Rep these 10 rows.

Papyrus Lace

Multiple of 8 + 1.

1st row (right side): K1, * yf, sl 1, k1, psso, k3, k2tog, yf, k1; rep from * to end.

2nd row and even rows: Purl.

3rd row: K1, *k1, yf, sl 1, k1, psso, k1, k2tog, yf, k2; rep from * to end.

5th row: K1, *k2, yf, sl 1, k2tog, yf, k3; rep from * to end.

7th row: Knit.

9th and 11th rows: K1, *k1, k2tog, yf, k1, yf, sl 1, k1, psso, k2; rep from * to end.

13th row: As 1st row.

15th row: As 3rd row.

17th row: As 5th row.

19th and 21st rows: As 9th row.

22nd row: P1, *yrn, p2tog, p3, p2tog tbl, yrn, p1; rep from * to end.

23rd row: K1, *k1, yrn, sl 1, k1, psso, k1, k2tog, yrn, k2; rep from * to end.

24th row: P1, *yrn, p2tog, yrn, p3tog, yrn, p2tog tbl, yrn, p1; rep from * to end.

25th row: K1, *k1, sl 1 k1 psso, yrn, k1, yrn, k2tog, k2; rep from * to end.

26th row: P1, *p1, p2tog, yrn, p1, yrn, p2tog tbl, p2; rep from * to end.

Rep from 23rd to 26th row.

Rep these 30 rows.

Lawn Hyacinths

Multiple of 6 + 2 sts for the rim on each edge.

1st row (right side): Knit.

2nd row: 1 edge st, k1, *p5tog, k1, p1, k1, p1, k1 into next st; rep from * to last 2 sts, k1, 1 edge st.

3rd and 5th rows: Purl.

4th row: 1 edge st, k1, *k1, p1, k1, p1, k1 into next st, p5tog; rep from * to last 2 sts, k1, 1 edge st.

6th row: Knit each st taking yarn 3 times around needle for each st.

Rep from row 2 to 6.

Slanting Stitch with Crochet

Multiple of 6 + 2 for the rim on each edge.

1st and 3rd rows (right side): Knit.

2nd row: Purl.

4th row: 1 edge st, *purl each st wrapping yarn 3 times around needle each time; rep from * to last st, 1 edge st.

5th row: 1 edge st, *slip next 3 sts onto cable needle and hold at front of work, k3, k3 sts from cable needle; rep from * to last st, 1 edge st.

6th and 7th rows: Knit.

8th row: Purl.

Rep rows 1 to 8.

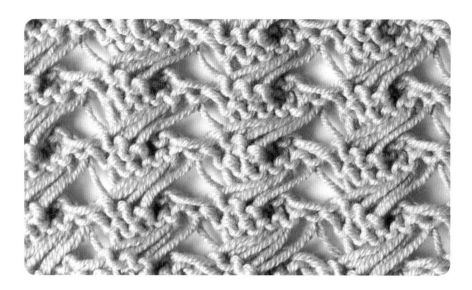

Extended Open-Work Stitches

Multiple of 6 + 2 st for the rim on each edge.

1st row (right side): Knit.

2nd row: I edge st, *knit each st wrapping yarn around needle 3 times; rep from * to last st , k1.

3rd row: I edge st, *slip next 3 sts onto cable needle and leave at back of work, k3, k3 sts from cable needle; rep from * to last st, I edge st.

4th row: Knit.

Rep these 4 rows.

Leafy Trellis

Multiple of 10 + 3.

1st row: Edge st, *k1 twisted, p1, K1B, p1, k1 twisted, p1, k1 twisted, k1 twisted, p1; rep from * to last st, twisted, edge st.

2nd row: Edge st, p1 twisted, *k1, p1 twisted, k1, p1 twisted, k1, p1 twisted, k1, p3, p1 twisted; rep from * to last st, edge st.

3rd row: Edge st, *k1 twisted, p1 (thread behind work), k2tog and draw sl st over, thro.o., p1, k1 twisted, p1, k1 twisted, p1, k1 twisted, p1; rep from * to last 2 sts, k1 twisted, edge st.

4th row: As 2nd row.

5th row: As 3rd row.

6th row: As 2nd row.

7th row: As 3rd row.

It's quite common to forget to make a yarnover when knitting. If you've forgotten to pass a slipped stitch, work it on the wrong side when you come to the decreased stitch.

Mesh Pattern

Odd number of sts.

1st row: K1, *yo, k2tog; rep from * to end.

2nd row: Purl.

3rd row: *Sl 1, k1, psso, yo; rep from * to last st, k1.

4th row: Purl.

Rep these 4 rows.

Mimosa Shoot

Multiple of 20.

1st row (right side): K6, yf, sl 1, k1, psso, k2, MB [k1, p1, k1, p1 into next st, turn, k4, turn, sl st purlwise, p3tog, psso], k9.

2nd and every alt row: Purl.

3rd row: K8, yf, sl 1, k1, psso, k2, MB, k8.

5th row: K10, yf, sl 1, k1, psso, k2, MB, k5.

7th row: K9, MB, k2, yf, sl 1, k1, psso, k2, MB, k3.

9th row: K7, MB, k2, k2tog, yf, k2, yf, sl 1, k1, psso, k2, MB, k1.

11th row: K5, MB, k2, k2tog, yf, k6, yf, sl 1, k1, psso, k2.

13th row: K3, MB, k2, k2tog, yf, k12.

15th row: K1, MB, k2, k2tog, yf, k2, MB, k11.

17th row: K2, k2tog, yf, k2, yf, sl 1, k1, psso, k2, MB, k9.

19th row: K8, yf, sl 1, k1, psso, k2 MB, k7.

20th row: Purl.

Rep rows 5 to 20.

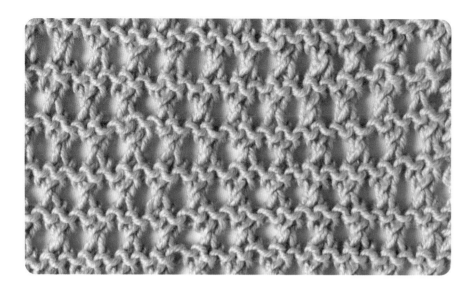

Ridged Eyelet Stitch

Multiple of 2.

1st, 2nd and 3rd rows: Knit.

4th row (wrong side): P1, *yrn, p2tog; rep from * to last st, p1.

5th, 6th and 7th rows: Knit.

8th row: P1, *p2tog, yrn; rep from * to last st, p1.

Rep these 8 rows.

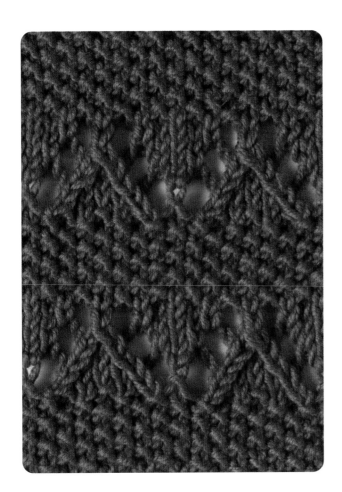

Lace and Moss Stitch

Multiple of 8 + 1.

Work 8 rows in Moss St.

Lace pattern:

1st row: K1, *yfon, sl 1, k1, psso, k3, k2tog, yfon, k1; rep from * to end.

2nd and every alt row: Purl.

3rd row: *K2, yfon, sl 1, k1, psso, k1, k2tog, yfon, k1; rep from * to last st, k1.

5th row: *K3, yfon, sl 1, k2tog, psso, yfon, k2; rep from * to last st, k1.

6th row: Purl.

Rep these 14 rows.

Vertical Slit Cables

Panel of 6 knit sts on an 8 st reverse St st background.

1st row (right side): P8, *k6, p8; rep from * to end.

2nd row: K8, *p6, k8; rep from * to end.

3rd row: P8, *sl 3 sts to cable needle and hold to back, k3, k3 from cable needle, p8; rep from * to end.

4th row: As 2nd row.

5th row: P8, k3, *k3, p8, k3; rep from *, end p8.

6th to 13th rows: Work each segment separately for these 8 rows.

14th row: Rejoin all segments to work across all sts as on row 2.

Rep rows 3 to 14 for vertical slit cables.

Slanting Eyelet Rib

Multiple of 8.

1st row: K3, p2, k2tog, yfwd,C2b, p1.

2nd row: K2, p3, k2, p3.

3rd row: K3, p1, k2tog, yfwd, C2b, p2.

4th row: K2, p4, k1, p3.

5th row: K3, k2tog, yfwd, C2b, k1, p2.

6th row: K2, p8.

7th row: K2, k2tog, yfwd, C2b, k2, p2.

8th row: K2, p8.

9th row: K1, k2tog, yfwd, C2b, k3, p2.

10th row: K2, p3, k1,pP4.

11th row: K2tog, yfwd, C2b, p1, k3, p2.

12th row: K2, p3, k2, p3.

2 x 2 Rib with Slits

Multiple of 26 + 12.

1st, 3rd and 5th rows (right side): P2, *k2, p2; rep from * to end.

2nd, 4th and 6th rows: K2, *p2, k2; rep from * to end.

7th row: P2, k10, [p2, k2] 3 times, p2, k10, p2.

8th row: K14, [p2, k2] 3 times, k12.

9th row: P14, [k2, p2] 2 times, k2, p14.

10th row: K2, [yo, p1] 10 times, [k2, p2] 3 times, k2, [yo, p1] 10 times, k2.

11th row: P2, [p next st letting extra yo drop from needle] 10 times, [p2, k2] 3 times, p2, [p next st letting extra yo drop from needle] 10 times, p2.

12th row: As 8th row.

13th row: As 7th row.

14th, 16th and 18th rows: As 2nd, 4th and 6th rows.

15th and 17th rows: As 3rd and 5th rows.

19th row: P2. [k2, p2] 3 times, k10, p2, [k2, p2] 3 times.

20th row: [K2, p2] 3 times, k14, [p2, k2] 3 times.

21st row: [P2, k2] 3 times, p14, [k2, p2] 3 times.

22nd row: K2, [p2, k2] 3 times, [yo, p1] 10 times, k2, [p2, k2] 3 times.

23rd row: [P2, k2] 3 times, p2, [p next st letting extra yo drop from needle] 10 times, [p2, k2] 3 times, p2.

24th row: As 20th row.

25th row: As 19th row.

Rep rows 2 to 25.

Spiral Cables

Multiple of 6 + 2.

1st row: K1 (selvedge st), *p1, k5; rep from * to last st, k1 (selvedge st).

2nd row: K1, *p5, k1; rep from * to last st, k1.

3rd row: K1, *yo, p1, k1, ssk, k2; rep from * to last st, k1.

4th row: K1, *p4, k1, p1; rep from * to last st, k1.

5th row: K1, *yo, p2, k1, ssk, k1; rep from * to last st, k1.

6th row: K1, *p3, k2, p1; rep from * to last st, k1.

7th row: K1, *yo, p3, k1, ssk; rep from * to last st, k1.

8th row: K1, *p2, k3, p1; rep from * to last st, k1.

Rep these 8 rows.

When slipping the first and last stitch of each row, be careful when you turn your work to avoid having a slipped loop down the side of your project.

Pucker Cable

Multiple of 5 + 3.

1st row (right side): *P1, k1 tbl, p1, k2; rep from * to last 3 sts, p1, k1 tbl, p1.

2nd row: K1, p1 tbl, k1, *p2, k1, p1 tbl, k1; rep from * to end.

3rd row: *P1, k1 tbl, p1, k1, yo, k1; rep from *, end p1, k1 tbl, p1.

4th row: K1, p1 tbl, k1, *p3, k1, p1 tbl, k1; rep from * to end.

5th row: *P1, k1 tbl, p1, k3, pass the 3rd st on RH needle over the centre 2 sts; rep from *, end p1, k1 tbl, p1.

Rep rows 2 to 5 for pattern st.

Open-Work Ladder Stitch

Multiple of 10 + 6.

1st row (wrong side): P6, *k2tog tbl, wind yarn twice around needle, k2tog, p6; rep from * to end.

2nd row: K6, *p1, p into first made st and k into the second st, p1, k6; rep from * to end.

Rep these 2 rows.

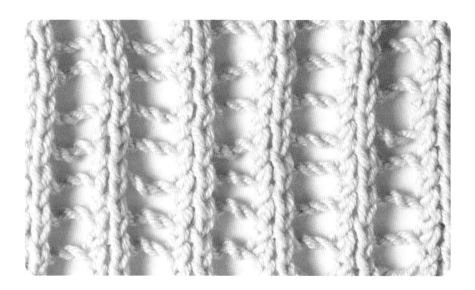

Simple Lace

Multiple of 4 + 2.

1st row: K1, *k2tog, yon twice, k2tog; rep from * to last st, k1.

2nd row: P1, *p2, k1, p1, rep from * to last st, p1.

Rep these 2 rows.

Embossed Leaf Pattern

Multiple of 7 + 6.

Note: sts should only be counted after the 15th and 16th rows of this pattern.

1st row (right side): P6, *yon, k1, yfrn, p6; rep from * to end.

2nd row: K6, *p3, k6; rep from * to end.

3rd row: P6, *[k1, yf] twice, k1, p6; rep from * to end.

4th row: K6, *p5, k6; rep from * to end.

5th row: P6, *k2, yf, k1, yf, k2, p6; rep from * to end.

6th row: K6, *p7, k6; rep from * to end.

7th row: P6, *k3, yf, k1, yf, k3, p6; rep from * to end.

8th row: K6, *p9, k6; rep from * to end.

9th row: P6, *sl 1, k1, psso, k5, k2tog, p6; rep from * to end.

10th row: K6, *p7, k6; rep from * to end.

11th row: P6, *sl 1, k1, psso, k3, k2tog, p6; rep from * to end.

12th row: K6, *p5, k6; rep from * to end.

13th row: P6, *sl 1, k1, psso, k1, k2tog, p6; rep from * to end.

14th row: K6, *p3, k6; rep from * to end.

15th row: P6, *sl 1, k2tog, psso, p6; rep from * to end.

16th row: Knit.

17th row: Purl.

18th, 19th, and 20th rows: Rep the last 2 rows once more, then the 16th row again.

Rep these 20 rows.

Bluebell Insertion

Multiple of 8.

1st row (right side): P2, [k1, p2] twice.

2nd row: K2, [p1, k2] twice.

3rd and 4th rows: Rep the last 2 rows once more.

5th row: P1, yon, sl 1, k1, psso, p2, k2tog, yfrn, p1.

6th row: K1, p2, k2, p2, k1.

7th row: P2, yon, sl 1, k1, psso, k2tog, yfrn, p2.

8th row: K2, p4, k2.

Rep these 8 rows.

Use a 'lifeline' or a thread that is run through all the stitches on a plain row so that if you make a mistake, you can rip out to the lifeline.

Eyelet Twist Panel

Multiple of 13.

1st and every alt row (wrong side): Purl.

2nd row: K1, [yf, sl 1, k1, psso] twice, k3, [k2tog, yf] twice, k1.

4th row: K2, [yf, sl 1, k1, psso] twice, k1, [k2tog, yf] twice, k2.

6th row: K3, yf, sl 1, k1, psso, yf, sl 1, k2tog, psso, yf, k2tog, yf, k3.

8th row: K4, yf, sl 1, k2tog, psso, yf, k2tog, yf, k4.

10th row: K4, [k2tog, yf] twice, k5.

12th row: K3, [k2tog, yf] twice, k1, yf, sl 1, k1, psso, k3.

14th row: K2, [k2tog, yf] twice, k1, [yf, sl 1, k1, psso] twice, k2.

16th row: K1, [k2tog, yf] twice, k3, [yf, sl 1, k1, psso] twice, k1.

18th row: [K2tog, yf] twice, k5, [yf, sl 1, k1, psso] twice.

Rep these 18 rows.

Tulip Bud Panel

Worked over 33 sts on a background of garter st.

1st row (wrong side): K16, p1, k16.

2nd row: K14, k2tog, yf, k1, yf, sl 1, k1, psso, k14.

3rd row: K14, p5, k14.

4th row: K13, k2tog, yf, k3, yf, sl 1, k1, psso, k13.

5th row: K13, p7, k13.

6th row: K12, [k2tog, yf] twice, k1, [yf, sl 1, k1, psso] twice, k12.

7th row: K12, p9, k12.

8th row: K11, [k2tog, yf] twice, k3, [yf, sl 1, k1, psso] twice, k11.

9th row: K11, p4, k1, p1, k1, p4, k11.

10th row: K10, [k2tog, yf] twice, k5, [yf, sl 1, k1, psso] twice, k10.

11th row: K10, p4, k2, p1, k2, p4, k10.

12th row: K9, [k2tog, yf] twice, k3, yf, k1, yf, k3, [yf, sl 1, k1, psso] twice, k9. (35 sts)

13th row: K9, p4, k3, p3, k3, p4, k9.

14th row: K1, yf, sl 1, k1, psso, k5, [k2tog, yf] twice, k5, yf, k1, yf, k5, [yf, sl 1, k1, psso] twice, k5, k2tog, yf, k1. (37 sts)

15th row: K1, p2, k5, p4, k4, p5, k4, p4, k5, p2, k1.

16th row: K2, yf, sl 1, k1, psso, k3, [k2tog, yf] twice, k7, yf, k1, yf, k7, [yf, sl 1, k1, psso] twice, k3, k2tog, yf, k2. (39 sts)

17th row: K2, p2, k3, p4, k5, p7, k5, p4, k3, p2, k2.

18th row: K3, yf, sl 1, k1, psso, k1, [k2tog, yf] twice, k1, k2tog, yf, k3. (41 sts)

19th row: K3, p2, k1, p4, k6, p9, k6, p4, k1, p2, k3.

20th row: K4, yf, sl 1, k2tog, psso, yf, k2tog, yf, k7, sl 1, k1, psso, k5, k2tog, k7, yf, sl 1, k1, psso, yf, k3tog, yf, k4. (39 sts)

21st row: K4, p5, k7, p7, k7, p5, k4.

22nd row: K16, sl 1, k1, psso, k3, k2tog, k16. (37 sts)

23rd row: K16, p5, k16.

24th row: K16, sl 1, k1, psso, k1, k2tog, k16. (35 sts)

25th row: K16, p3, k16.

26th row: K16, sl 1, k2tog, psso, k16. (33 sts)

27th row: As 1st row.

Rep these 27 rows.

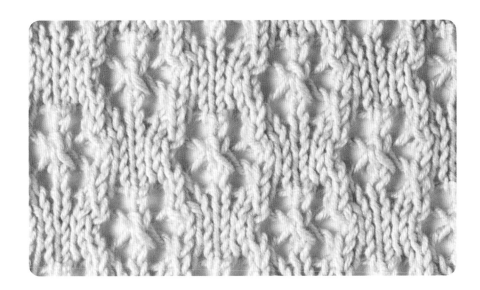

Lacy Stars

Multiple of 6 + 3.

1st row (right side): Purl.

2nd row: Knit.

3rd row: Purl.

4th row: K1, p3tog, [k1, p1, k1, p1, k1] into next st, *p5tog, [k1, p1, k1, p1, k1] into next st; rep from * to last 4 sts, p3tog, k1.

5th row: Purl.

6th row: K1, [k1, p1, k1] into next st, p5tog, *[k1, p1, k1, p1, k1] into next st, p5tog; rep from * to last 2 sts, [k1, p1, k1] into next st, k1.

7th row: Purl.

8th row: Knit.

Rep these 8 rows.

Dewdrop Pattern

Multiple of 6 + 1.

1st row (wrong side): K2, *p3, k3; rep from * to last 5 sts, p3, k2.

2nd row: P2, *k3, p3; rep from * to last 5 sts, k3, p2.

3rd row: As 1st row.

4th row: K2, *yf, sl 1, k2tog, psso, yf, k3; rep from * to last 5 sts, yf, sl 1, k2tog, psso, yf, k2.

5th row: As 2nd row.

6th row: K2, *p3, k3; rep from * to last 5 sts, p3, k2.

7th row: As 2nd row.

8th row: K2tog, *yf, k3, yf, sl 1, k2tog, psso; rep from * to last 5 sts, yf, k3, yf, sl 1, k1, psso.

Rep these 8 rows.

Fern Lace

Multiple of 9 + 4.

1st row (wrong side): Purl.

2nd row: K3, *yf, k2, sl 1, k1, psso, k2tog, k2, yf, k1; rep from * to last st, k1.

3rd row: Purl.

4th row: K2, *yf, k2, sl 1, k1, psso, k2tog, k2, yf, k1; rep from * to last 2 sts, k2.

Rep these 4 rows.

Filigree Cables
Pattern Lace

Multiple of 12 + 8.

1st row (right side): P2, *k2, yf, k2tog, p2; rep from * to end.

2nd row: K2, *p2, yrn, p2tog, k2; rep from * to end.

Rep the last 2 rows twice more.

7th row: P2, k2, yf, k2tog, p2, *C4F, p2, k2, yf, k2tog, p2; rep from * to end.

8th row: As 2nd row.

Rep the 1st and 2nd rows 3 times more.

15th row: P2, C4F, p2, *k2, yf, k2tog, p2, C4F, p2; rep from * to end.

16th row: As 2nd row.

Rep these 16 rows.

After knitting a swatch, some knitters wash it to avoid any irreversible damage to the project that may occur in the washing machine.

Falling Leaves

Multiple of 10 + 3.

1st row (right side): K1, k2tog, k3, *yf, k1, yf, k3, sl 1, k2tog, psso, k3; rep from * to last 7 sts, yf, k1, yf, k3, sl 1, k1, psso, k1.

2nd and every alt row: Purl.

3rd row: K1, k2tog, k2, *yf, k3, yf, k2, sl 1, k2tog, psso, k2; rep from * to last 8 sts, yf, k3, yf, k2, sl 1, k1, psso, k1.

5th row: K1, k2tog, k1, *yf, k5, yf, k1, sl 1, k2tog, psso, k1; rep from * to last 9 sts, yf, k5, yf, k1, sl 1, k1, psso, k1.

7th row: K1, k2tog, yf, k7, *yf, sl 1, k2tog, psso, yf, k7; rep from * to last 3 sts, yf, sl 1, k1, psso, k1.

9th row: K2, yf, k3, *sl 1, k2tog, psso, k3, yf, k1, yf, k3; rep from * to last 8 sts, sl 1, k2tog, psso, k3, yf, k2.

11th row: K3, yf, k2, *sl 1, k2tog, psso, k2, yf, k3, yf, k2; rep from * to last 8 sts, sl 1, k2tog, psso, k2, yf, k3.

13th row: K4, yf, k1, *sl 1, k2tog, psso, k1, yf, k5, yf, k1; rep from * to last 8 sts, sl 1, k2tog, psso, k1, yf, k4.

15th row: K5, *yf, sl 1, k2tog, psso, yf, k7; rep from * to last 8 sts, yf, sl 1, k2tog, psso, yf, k5.

16th row: Purl.

Rep these 16 rows.

Fern Diamonds

Multiple of 10 + 1.

1st row (right side): K3, *k2tog, yf, k1, yf, sl 1, k1, psso, k5; rep from * to last 8 sts, k2tog, yf, k1, yf, sl 1, k1, psso, k3.

2nd and every alt row: Purl.

3rd row: K2, *k2tog, [k1, yf] twice, k1, sl 1, k1, psso, k3; rep from * to last 9 sts, k2tog, [k1, yf] twice, k1, sl 1, k1, psso, k2.

5th row: K1, *k2tog, k2, yf, k1, yf, k2, sl 1, k1, psso, k1; rep from * to end.

7th row: K2tog, *k3, yf, k1, yf, k3, sl 1, k2tog, psso; rep from * to last 9 sts, k3, yf, k1, yf, k3, sl 1, k1, psso.

9th row: K1, *yf, sl 1, k1, psso, k5, k2tog, yf, k1; rep from * to end.

11th row: K1, *yf, k1, sl 1, k1, psso, k3, k2tog, k1, yf, k1; rep from * to end.

13th row: K1, *yf, k2, sl 1, k1, psso, k1, k2tog, k2, yf, k1; rep from * to end.

15th row: K1, *yf, k3, sl 1, k2tog, psso, k3, yf, k1; rep from * to end.

16th row: Purl.

Rep these 16 rows.

Cable and Lace Check

Multiple of 12 + 8.

1st row (wrong side): K2, p2tog, yrn, p2, k2, *p4, k2, p2tog, yrn, p2, k2; rep from * to end.

2nd row: P2, k2tog, yf, k2, p2, *k4, p2, k2tog, yf, k2, p2; rep from * to end.

3rd row: As 1st row.

4th row: P2, k2tog, yf, k2, p2, *C4B, p2, k2tog, yf, k2, p2; rep from * to end.

5th, 6th, and 7th rows: As 1st, 2nd and 3rd rows.

8th row: P2, *C4B, p2; rep from * to end.

9th row: K2, p4, k2, *p2tog, yrn, p2, k2, p4, k2; rep from * to end.

10th row: P2, k4, p2, *k2tog, yf, k2, p2, k4, p2; rep from * to end.

11th row: As 9th row.

12th row: P2, C4B, p2, *k2tog, yf, k2, p2, C4B, p2; rep from * to end.

13th, 14th, and 15th rows: As 9th, 10th and 11th rows.

16th row: As 8th row.

Rep these 16 rows.

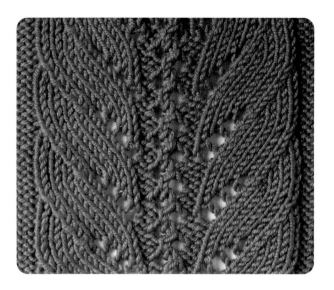

Spiral and Eyelet Panel

Worked across 24 sts on a background of reverse St st.

1st row (right side): K3, k2tog, k4, yfrn, p2, yon, k2tog, p2, yon, k4, sl 1, k1, psso, k3.

2nd and every alt row: P9, k2, p2, k2, p9.

3rd row: K2, k2tog, k4, yf, k1, p2, k2tog, yfrn, p2, k1, yf, k4, sl 1, k1, psso, k2.

5th row: K1, k2tog, k4, yf, k2, p2, yon, k2tog, p2, k2, yf, k4, sl 1, k1, psso, k1.

7th row: K2tog, k4, yf, k3, p2, k2tog, yfrn, p2, k3, yf, k4, sl 1, k1, psso.

8th row: P9, k2, p2, k2, p9.

Rep these 8 rows.

Ornamental Parasols

Multiple of 18 + 1.

Note: Sts should only be counted after the 5th, 6th, 11th, 12th, 13th, 14th, 25th, 26th, 27th and 28th rows.

1st row (right side): K1, *[p2, k1] twice, yf, k2tog, yf, k1, yf, sl 1, k1, psso, yf, [k1, p2] twice, k1; rep from * to end.

2nd row: [P1, k2] twice, p9, *k2, [p1, k2] 3 times, p9; rep from * to last 6 sts, [k2, p1] twice.

3rd row: K1, *[p2, k1] twice, yf, k2tog, yf, k3, yf, sl 1, k1, psso, yf, [k1, p2] twice, k1; rep from * to end.

4th row: [P1, k2] twice, p11, *k2, [p1, k2] 3 times, p11; rep from * to last 6 sts, [k2, p1] twice.

5th row: K1, *[p2tog, k1] twice, yf, k2tog, yf, sl 1, k1, psso, k1, k2tog, yf, sl 1, k1, psso, yf, [k1, p2tog] twice, k1; rep from * to end.

6th row: [P1, k1] twice, p11, *k1, [p1, k1] 3 times, p11; rep from * to last 4 sts, [k1, p1] twice.

7th row: K1, *[p1, k1] twice, yf, k2tog, yf, knit into back of next st (called KB1), yf, sl 1, k2tog, psso, yf, KB1, yf, sl 1, k1, psso, yf, [k1, p1] twice, k1; rep from * to end.

8th row: [P1, k1] twice, p13, *k1, [p1, k1] 3 times, p13; rep from * to last 4 sts, [k1, p1] twice.

9th row: K1, *[k2tog] twice, yf, k2tog, yf, k3, yf, k1, yf, k3, yf, sl 1, k1, psso, yf, [sl 1, k1, psso] twice, k1; rep from * to end.

10th row: Purl.

11th row: K1, *[k2tog, yf] twice, sl 1, k1, psso, k1, k2tog, yf, k1, yf, sl 1, k1, psso, k1, k2tog, [yf, sl 1, k1, psso] twice, k1; rep from * to end.

12th row: Purl.

13th row: [K2tog, yf] twice, KB1, yf, sl 1, k2tog, psso, yf, k3, yf, sl 1, k2tog, psso, yf, KB1, yf, sl 1, k1, psso, *yf, sl 1, k2tog, psso, yf, k2tog, yf, KB1, yf, sl 1, k2tog, psso, yf, k3, yf, sl 1, k2tog, psso, yf, KB1, yf, sl 1, k1, psso; rep from * to last 2 sts, yf, sl 1, k1, psso.

14th row: Purl.

15th row: K1, *yf, sl 1, k1, psso, yf, [k1, p2] 4 times, k1, yf, k2tog, yf, k1; rep from * to end.

16th row: P5, [k2, p1] 3 times, k2, *p9, [k2, p1] 3 times, k2; rep from * to last 5 sts, p5.

17th row: K2, yf, sl 1, k1, psso, yf, [k1, p2] 4 times, k1, yf, k2tog, *yf, k3, yf, sl 1, k1, psso, yf, [k1, p2] 4 times, k1, yf, k2tog; rep from * to last 2 sts, yf, k2.

18th row: P6, [k2, p1] 3 times, k2, *p11, [k2, p1] 3 times, k2; rep from * to last 6 sts, p6.

19th row: K1, *k2tog, yf, sl 1, k1, psso, yf, [k1, p2tog] 4 times, k1, yf, k2tog, yf, sl 1, k1, psso, k1; rep from * to end.

20th row: P6, [k1, p1] 3 times, k1, *p11, [k1, p1] 3 times, k1; rep from * to last 6 sts, p6.

21st row: K2tog, yf, KB1, yf, sl 1, k1, psso, yf, [k1, p1] 4 times, k1, yf, k2tog, yf, KB1, *yf, sl 1, k2tog, psso, yf, KB1, yf, sl 1, k1, psso, yf, [k1, p1] 4 times, k1, yf, k2tog, yf, KB1; rep from * to last 2 sts, yf, sl 1, k1, psso.

22nd row: P7, [k1, p1] 3 times, k1, *p13, [k1, p1] 3 times, k1; rep from * to last 7 sts, p7.

23rd row: K1, *yf, k3, yf, sl 1, k1, psso, yf, [sl 1, k1, psso] twice, k1, [k2tog] twice, yf, k2tog, yf, k3, yf, k1; rep from * to end.

24th row: Purl.

25th row: K1, *yf, sl 1, k1, psso, k1, k2tog, [yf, sl 1, k1, psso] twice, k1, [k2tog, yf] twice, sl 1, k1, psso, k1, k2tog, yf, k1; rep from * to end.

26th row: Purl.

27th row: K2, yf, sl 1, k2tog, psso, yf, KB1, yf, sl 1, k1, psso, yf, sl 1, k2tog, psso, yf, k2tog, yf, KB1, yf, sl 1, k2tog, psso, *yf, k3, yf, sl 1, k2tog, psso, yf, KB1, yf, sl 1, k1, psso, yf, sl 1, k2tog, psso, yf, k2tog, yf, KB1, yf, sl 1, k2tog, psso; rep from * to last 2 sts, yf, k2.

28th row: Purl.

Rep these 28 rows.

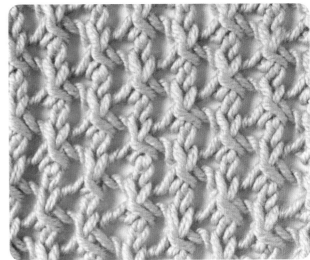

Garter Stitch Eyelet Chevron

Multiple of 9 + 1.

1st row (right side): K1, *yf, sl 1, k1, psso, k4, k2tog, yf, k1; rep from * to end.

2nd row: P2, *k6, p3; rep from * to last 8 sts, k6, p2.

3rd row: K2, *yf, sl 1, k1, psso, k2, k2tog, yf, k3; rep from * to last 8 sts, yf, sl 1, k1, psso, k2, k2tog, yf, k2.

4th row: P3, *k4, p5; rep from * to last 7 sts, k4, p3.

5th row: K3, *yf, sl 1, k1, psso, k2tog, yf, k5; rep from * to last 7 sts, yf, sl 1, k1, psso, k2tog, yf, k3.

6th row: P4, *k2, p7; rep from * to last 6 sts, k2, p4.

Rep these 6 rows.

Cell Stitch

Multiple of 4 + 3.

1st row (right side): K2, *yf, sl 1, k2tog, psso, yf, k1; rep from * to last st, k1.

2nd row: Purl.

3rd row: K1, k2tog, yf, k1, *yf, sl 1, k2tog, psso, yf, k1; rep from * to last 3 sts, yf, sl 1, k1, psso, k1.

4th row: Purl.

Rep these 4 rows.

Peacock Plumes

Multiple of 16 + 1.

1st and 3rd rows (wrong side): Purl.

2nd row: Knit.

4th row: [K1, yf] 3 times, [sl 1, k1, psso] twice, sl 2, k1, p2sso, [k2tog] twice, *yf, [k1, yf] 5 times, [sl 1, k1, psso] twice, sl 2, k1, p2sso, [k2tog] twice; rep from * to last 3 sts, [yf, k1] 3 times.

Rep the last 4 rows 3 times more.

17th and 19th rows: Purl.

18th row: Knit.

20th row: [K2tog] 3 times, [yf, k1] 5 times, *yf, [sl 1, k1, psso] twice, sl 2, k1, p2sso, [k2tog] twice, [yf, k1] 5 times; rep from * to last 6 sts, yf, [sl 1, k1, psso] 3 times.

Rep the last 4 rows 3 times more.

Rep these 32 rows.

When you make a mistake, correct it by ripping back stitch by stitch.

Crowns I

Multiple of 5.

Work 4 rows in garter stitch.

5th row: K1, *k1 winding yarn around needle 3 times; rep from * to end.

6th row: *Sl 5 sts purlwise dropping extra loops, return these 5 sts to LH needle then work into these 5 sts together as follows: k1, [p1, k1] twice; rep from * to end.

Work 2 rows in garter stitch.

Rep these 8 rows.

Little Arrowhead

Multiple of 6 + 1.

1st row (right side): K1, *yf, sl 1, k1, psso, k1, k2tog, yf, k1; rep from * to end.

2nd row: Purl.

3rd row: K2, *yf, sl 1, k2tog, psso, yf, k3; rep from * to last 5 sts, yf, sl 1, k2tog, psso, yf, k2.

4th row: Purl.

Rep these 4 rows.

Candelabra Panel

Worked over 13 sts on a background of St st.

1st row (right side): Knit.

2nd and every alt row: Purl.

3rd row: Knit.

5th row: K4, k2tog, yf, k1, yf, sl 1, k1, psso, k4.

7th row: K3, k2tog, yf, k3, yf, sl 1, k1, psso, k3.

9th row: K2, [k2tog, yf] twice, k1, [yf, sl 1, k1, psso] twice, k2.

11th row: K1, [k2tog, yf] twice, k3, [yf, sl 1, k1, psso] twice, k1.

13th row: [K2tog, yf] 3 times, k1, [yf, sl 1, k1, psso] 3 times.

14th row: Purl.

Rep these 14 rows.

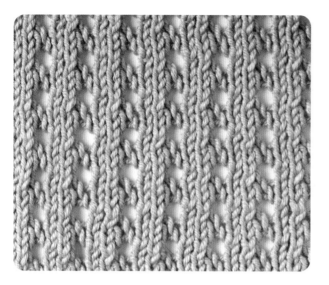

Eyelets

Multiple of 3 + 2.

1st and 2nd rows: Work 2 rows in St st, starting knit.

3rd row (right side): K2, *yf, k2tog, k1; rep from * to end.

4th row: Purl.

Rep these 4 rows.

Foaming Waves

Multiple of 12 + 1.

1st, 2nd, 3rd, and 4th rows: Knit 4 rows.

5th row (right side): K1, *[k2tog] twice, [yf, k1] 3 times, yf, [sl 1, k1, psso] twice, k1; rep from * to end.

6th row: Purl.

7th, 8th, 9th, 10th, 11th, and 12th rows: Rep the last 2 rows 3 times more.

Rep these 12 rows.

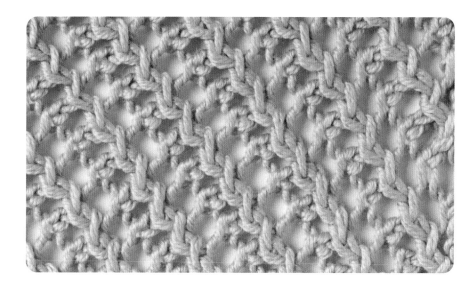

Diagonal Openwork

Multiple of 4 + 2.

1st row (right side): *K1, yf, sl 1, k2tog, psso, yf; rep from * to last 2 sts, k2.

2nd and every alt row: Purl.

3rd row: K2, *yf, sl 1, k2tog, psso, yf, k1; rep from * to end.

5th row: K2tog, yf, k1, yf, *sl 1, k2tog, psso, yf, k1, yf; rep from * to last 3 sts, sl 1, k1, psso, k1.

7th row: K1, k2tog, yf, k1, yf, *sl 1, k2tog, psso, yf, k1, yf; rep from * to last 2 sts, sl 1, k1, psso.

8th row: Purl.

Rep these 8 rows.

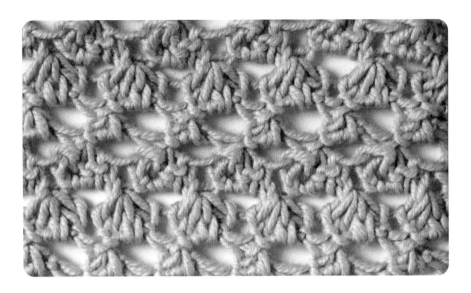

Grand Eyelets

Multiple of 4.

Note: Sts should not be counted after the 1st row.

1st row: P2, *yrn, p4tog; rep from * to last 2 sts, p2.

2nd row: K3, [k1, p1, k1] into next st, *k1, [k1, p1, k1] into next st; rep from * to last 2 sts, k2.

3rd row: Knit.

Rep these 3 rows.

Cast on slowly to keep the tension as even as possible.

Leafy Lace

Multiple of 10 + 1.

1st row (right side): KB1, *p9, KB1; rep from * to end.

2nd row: P1, *k9, p1; rep from * to end.

Rep the last 2 rows once more.

5th row: KB1, *p2, p2tog, yon, KB1, yfrn, p2tog, p2, KB1; rep from * to end.

6th row: P1, *k4, PB1, k4, p1; rep from * to end.

7th row: KB1, *p1, p2tog, yon, [KB1] 3 times, yfrn, p2tog, p1, KB1; rep from * to end.

8th row: P1, *k3, [PB1] 3 times, k3, p1; rep from * to end.

9th row: KB1, *p2tog, yon, [KB1] 5 times, yfrn, p2tog, KB1; rep from * to end.

10th row: P1, *k2, [PB1] 5 times, k2, p1; rep from * to end.

11th row: KB1, *p1, yon, [KB1] twice, sl 1, k2tog, psso, [KB1] twice, yfrn, p1, KB1; rep from * to end.

12th row: As 10th row.

13th row: KB1, *p2, yon, KB1, sl 1, k2tog, psso, KB1, yfrn, p2, KB1; rep from * to end.

14th row: As 8th row.

15th row: KB1, *p3, yon, sl 1, k2tog, psso, yfrn, p3, KB1; rep from * to end.

16th row: As 6th row.

Rep these 16 rows.

Braided Openwork

Multiple of 2.

1st row (wrong side): Purl.

2nd row (right side): K1, *sl 1, k1, psso, M1; rep from *
to last st, k1.

3rd row: Purl.

4th row: K1, *M1, k2tog; rep from * to last st, k1.

Rep these 4 rows.

Little Flowers

Multiple of 6 + 3.

1st row (right side): Knit.

2nd and every alt row: Purl.

3rd row: Knit.

5th row: *K4, yf, sl 1, k1, psso; rep from * to last 3 sts, k3.

7th row: K2, k2tog, yf, k1, yf, sl 1, k1, psso, *k1, k2tog, yf, k1, yf, sl 1, k1, psso; rep from * to last 2 sts, k2.

9th and 11th rows: Knit.

13th row: K1, yf, sl 1, k1, psso, *k4, yf, sl 1, k1, psso; rep from * to end.

15th row: K2, yf, sl 1, k1, psso, k1, k2tog, yf, *k1, yf, sl 1, k1, psso, k1, k2tog, yf; rep from * to last 2 sts, k2.

16th row: Purl.

Rep these 16 rows.

Bluebell Ribs

Multiple of 5 + 2.

1st row (right side): P2, *k3, p2; rep from * to end.

2nd row: K2, *p3, k2; rep from * to end.

Rep the last 2 rows once more.

5th row: P2, *yon, sl 1, k2tog, psso, yfrn, p2; rep from * to end.

6th row: As 2nd row.

Rep these 6 rows.

Little Fountain Pattern

Multiple of 4 + 1.

Note: Sts should only be counted after the 3rd and 4th rows.

1st row (right side): K1, *yf, k3, yf, k1; rep from * to end.

2nd row: Purl.

3rd row: K2, sl 1, k2tog, psso, *k3, sl 1, k2tog, psso; rep from * to last 2 sts, k2.

4th row: Purl.

Rep these 4 rows.

Meandering Cables with Eyelets

Multiple of 16 + 10.

Note: Sts should only be counted after the 1st, 14th, 15th and 28th rows.

1st row (wrong side): K2, *p6, k2; rep from * to end.

2nd row: P2, [k2tog, yf] twice, k2tog, *p2, k6, p2, [k2tog, yf] twice, k2tog; rep from * to last 2 sts, p2.

3rd row: K2, p5, k2, *p6, k2, p5, k2; rep from * to end.

4th row: P2, k1, [yf, k2tog] twice, p2, *C6F, p2, k1, [yf, k2tog] twice, p2; rep from * to end.

5th row: As 3rd row.

6th row: P2, k1, [yf, k2tog] twice, p2, *k6, p2, k1, [yf, k2tog] twice, p2; rep from * to end.

Rep the last 2 rows twice more, then 5th row again.

12th row: As 4th row.

13th row: As 3rd row.

14th row: P2, k2, yf, k1, yf, k2tog, p2, *k6, p2, k2, yf, k1, yf, k2tog, p2; rep from * to end.

15th row: As 1st row.

16th row: P2, k6, p2, *yb, sl 1, k1, psso, [yf, sl 1, k1, psso] twice, p2, k6, p2; rep from * to end.

17th row: K2, p6, k2, *p5, k2, p6, k2; rep from * to end.

18th row: P2, C6F, p2, *yb, [sl 1, k1, psso, yf] twice, k1, p2, C6F, p2; rep from * to end.

19th row: As 17th row.

20th row: P2, k6, p2, *yb, [sl 1, k1, psso, yf] twice, k1, p2, k6, p2; rep from * to end.

Rep the last 2 rows twice more, then 19th row again.

26th row: As 18th row.

27th row: As 17th row.

28th row: P2, k6, p2, *k2, yf, sl 1, k1, psso, yf, k1, p2, k6, p2; rep from * to end.

Rep these 28 rows.

Eyelet Panes

Multiple of 6 + 3.

Note: Sts should not be counted after the 3rd, 4th, 9th or 10th rows of this pattern.

1st row (right side): K2, *yf, sl 1, k1, psso, k1, k2tog, yf, k1; rep from * to last st, k1.

2nd and every alt row: Purl.

3rd row: K3, *yf, k3; rep from * to end.

5th row: K1, k2tog, *yf, sl 1, k1, psso, k1, k2tog, yf, sl 1, k2tog, psso; rep from * to last 8 sts, yf, sl 1, k1, psso, k1, k2tog, yf, sl 1, k1, psso, k1.

7th row: K2, *k2tog, yf, k1, yf, sl 1, k1, psso, k1; rep from * to last st, k1.

9th row: As 3rd row.

11th row: K2, *k2tog, yf, sl 1, k2tog, psso, yf, sl 1, k1, psso, k1; rep from * to last st, k1.

12th row: Purl.

Rep these 12 rows.

Butterfly Lace

Multiple of 8 + 7.

1st row (right side): K1, *k2tog, yf, k1, yf, sl 1, k1, psso, k3; rep from * to last 6 sts, k2tog, yf, k1, yf, sl 1, k1, psso, k1.

2nd row: P3, *sl 1 purlwise, p7; rep from * to last 4 sts, sl 1 purlwise, p3.

Rep the last 2 rows once more.

5th row: K5, *k2tog, yf, k1, yf, sl 1, k1, psso, k3; rep from * to last 2 sts, k2.

6th row: P7, *sl 1 purlwise, p7; rep from * to end.

Rep the last 2 rows once more.

Rep these 8 rows.

Lace Diamond Border

Multiple of 8.

1st row (right side): *K1, yf, k3, pass 3rd st on right-hand needle over first 2 sts; rep from * to end.

2nd and every alt row: Purl.

3rd row: Knit.

5th row: K3, *yf, sl 1, k1, psso, k6; rep from * to last 5 sts, yf, sl 1, k1, psso, k3.

7th row: K2, *[yf, sl 1, k1, psso] twice, k4; rep from * to last 6 sts, [yf, sl 1, k1, psso] twice, k2.

9th row: K1, *[yf, sl 1, k1, psso] 3 times, k2; rep from * to last 7 sts, [yf, sl 1, k1, psso] 3 times, k1.

11th row: As 7th row.

13th row: As 5th row.

15th row: Knit.

17th row: As 1st row.

18th row: Purl.

Bead Stitch

Multiple of 7.

1st row (right side): K1, k2tog, yf, k1, yf, sl 1, k1, psso, *k2, k2tog, yf, k1, yf, sl 1, k1, psso; rep from * to last st, k1.

2nd row: *P2tog tbl, yrn, p3, yrn, p2tog; rep from * to end.

3rd row: K1, yf, sl 1, k1, psso, k1, k2tog, yf, *k2, yf, sl 1, k1, psso, k1, k2tog, yf; rep from * to last st, k1.

4th row: P2, yrn, p3tog, yrn, *p4, yrn, p3tog, yrn; rep from * to last 2 sts, p2.

Rep these 4 rows.

Take the time to study a pattern to prevent making regrettable mistakes.

Cockleshells

Worked over 19 sts on a background of garter stitch.

1st row (right side): Knit.

2nd row: Knit.

3rd row: K1, yfrn, yrn, p2tog tbl, k13, p2tog, yrn, yon, k1.

4th row: K2, p1, k15, p1, k2.

5th and 6th rows: Knit.

7th row: K1, yfrn, yrn, p2tog tbl, [yrn] twice, p2tog tbl, k11, p2tog, [yrn] twice, p2tog, yrn, yon, k1.

8th row: [k2, p1] twice, k13, [p1, k2] twice.

9th row: Knit.

10th row: K5, k15 wrapping yarn 3 times around needle for each st, k5.

11th row: K1, yfrn, yrn, p2tog tbl, [yrn] twice, p2tog tbl, [yrn] twice, pass next 15 sts to right-hand needle dropping extra loops, pass same 15 sts back to left-hand needle and purl all 15 sts tog, [yrn] twice, p2tog, [yrn] twice, p2tog, yrn, yon, k1.

12th row: K1, p1, [k2, p1] twice, k3, [p1, k2] twice, p1, k1.

Rep these 12 rows.

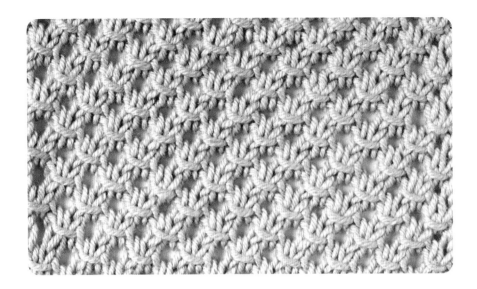

Knotted Openwork

Multiple of 3.

1st row (wrong side): Purl.

2nd row: K2, *yf, k3, with left-hand needle lift first of the 3 sts just knitted over the last 2; rep from * to last st, k1.

3rd row: Purl.

4th row: K1, *k3, with left-hand needle lift first of the 3 sts just knitted over the last 2, yf; rep from * to last 2 sts, k2.

Rep these 4 rows.

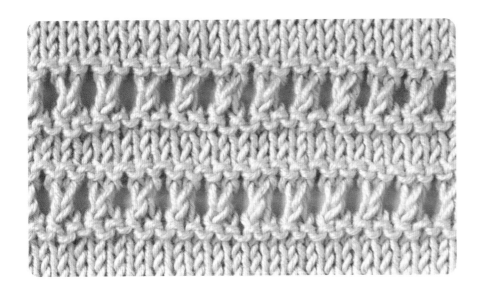

Ridged Eyelet Border

Multiple of 2 + 1.

Worked on a background of st st.

1st, 2nd and 3rd rows:: Knit.

4th row (wrong side): *P2tog, yrn; rep from * to last st,
p1.

5th, 6th and 7th rows: Knit.

8th row: Purl.

Rep the first 6 rows once more.

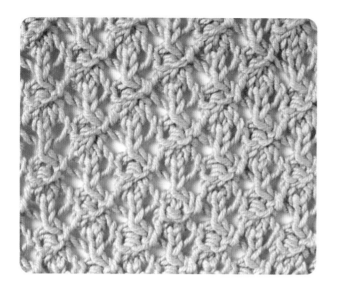

Lacy Lattice Stitch

Multiple of 6 + 1.

1st row (right side): K1, *yfrn, p1, p3tog, p1, yon, k1; rep from * to end.

2nd and every alt row: Purl.

3rd row: K2, yf, sl 1, k2tog, psso, yf, *k3, yf, sl 1, k2tog, psso, yf; rep from * to last 2 sts, k2.

5th row: P2tog, p1, yon, k1, yfrn, p1, *p3tog, p1, yon, k1, yfrn, p1; rep from * to last 2 sts, p2tog.

7th row: K2tog, yf, k3, yf, *sl 1, k2tog, psso, yf, k3, yf; rep from * to last 2 sts, sl 1, k1, psso.

8th row: Purl.

Rep these 8 rows.

Parasol Stitch

Worked over 17 sts on a background of St st.

Note: Sts should only be counted after the 11th and 12th rows of this pattern.

1st row (right side): Yf, k1, [p3, k1] 4 times, yf.

2nd and every alt row: Purl.

3rd row: K1, yf, k1, [p3, k1] 4 times, yf, k1.

5th row: K2, yf, k1, [p3, k1] 4 times, yf, k2.

7th row: K3, yf, k1, [p2tog, p1, k1] 4 times, yf, k3.

9th row: K4, yf, k1, [p2tog, k1] 4 times, yf, k4.

11th row: K5, yf, k1, [k3tog, k1] twice, yf, k5.

12th row: Purl.

Rep these 12 rows.

Frost Flower Pattern

Multiple of 34 + 2.

1st row (right side): K4, *k2tog, k4, yfrn, p2, [k2, yf, sl 1, k1, psso] 3 times, p2, yon, k4, sl 1, k1, psso, k6; rep from * but ending last rep with k4 instead of k6.

2nd row: P3, *p2tog tbl, p4, yrn, p1, k2, [p2, yrn, p2tog] 3 times, k2, p1, yrn, p4, p2tog, p4; rep from * but ending last rep with p3 instead of p4.

3rd row: K2, *k2tog, k4, yf, k2, p2, [k2, yf, sl 1, k1, psso] 3 times, p2, k2, yf, k4, sl 1, k1, psso, k2; rep from * to end.

4th row: P1, *p2tog tbl, p4, yrn, p3, k2, [p2, yrn, p2tog] 3 times, k2, p3, yrn, p4, p2tog; rep from * to last st, p1.

Rep the last 4 rows twice more.

13th row: K1, *yf, sl 1, k1, psso, k2, yf, sl 1, k1, psso, p2, yon, k4, sl 1, k1, psso, k6, k2tog, k4, yfrn, p2, k2, yf, sl 1, k1, psso, k2; rep from * but ending last rep with k3 instead of k2.

14th row: P1, *yrn, p2tog, p2, yrn, p2tog, k2, p1, yrn, p4, p2tog, p4, p2tog tbl, p4, yrn, p1, k2, p2, yrn, p2tog, p2; rep from * but ending last rep with p3 instead of p2.

15th row: K1, *yf, sl 1, k1, psso, k2, yf, sl 1, k1, psso, p2, k2, yf, k4, sl 1, k1, psso, k2, k2tog, k4, yf, k2, p2, k2, yf, sl 1, k1, psso, k2; rep from * but ending last rep with k3 instead of k2.

16th row: P1, *yrn, p2tog, p2, yrn, p2tog, k2, p3, yrn, p4, p2tog, p2tog tbl, p4, yrn, p3, k2, p2, yrn, p2tog, p2; rep from * but ending last rep with p3 instead of p2.

Rep the last 4 rows twice more.

Rep these 24 rows.

Little Shell Pattern

Multiple of 7 + 2.

1st row (right side): Knit.

2nd row: Purl.

3rd row: K2, *yfrn, p1, p3tog, p1, yon, k2; rep from * to end.

4th row: Purl.

Rep these 4 rows.

If and when you can, purchase an extra skein of yarn in the same dye lot – you may find that you need it.

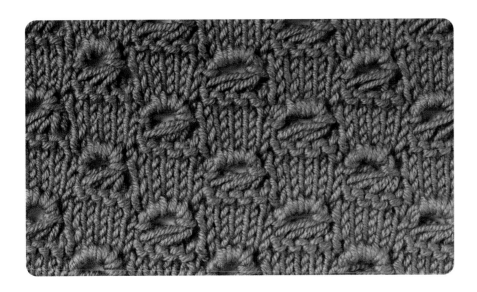

Crowns II

Multiple of 10 + 7.

Special Abbreviations: KW5 = knit 5 sts wrapping yarn 3 times around needle for each st.

Twist 5 = slip 5 sts purlwise dropping extra loops, return these 5 sts to left-hand needle, then k1, [p1, k1] twice into same 5 sts tog.

1st row: K6, KW5, *k5, KW5; rep from * to last 6 sts, k6.

2nd row: P6, Twist 5, *p5, Twist 5; rep from * to last 6 sts, p6.

3rd row: Knit.

4th row: K6, p5, *k5, p5; rep from * to last 6 sts, k6.

5th row: K1, KW5, *k5, KW5; rep from * to last st, k1.

6th row: P1, Twist 5, *p5, Twist 5; rep from * to last st, p1.

7th row: Knit.

8th row: K1, p5, *k5, p5; rep from * to last st, k1.

Rep these 8 rows.

Faggoted Panel

Worked over 9 sts on a St st background.

1st row (right side): P1, k1, k2tog, yf, k1, yf, k2tog tbl, k1, p1.

2nd row: K1, p7, k1.

3rd row: P1, k2tog, yf, k3, yf, k2tog tbl, p1.

4th row: As 2nd row.

Rep these 4 rows.

Tunnel Lace

Multiple of 3 + 2.

Note: Sts should only be counted after the 4th row of this pattern.

1st row (right side): P2, *yon, k1, yfrn, p2; rep from * to end.

2nd row: K2, *p3, k2; rep from * to end.

3rd row: P2, *k3, p2; rep from * to end.

4th row: K2, *p3tog, k2; rep from * to end.

Rep these 4 rows.

Bear Paw Panel

Worked over 23 sts on a background of St st.

1st row (right side): K2, [p4, k1] 3 times, p4, k2.

2nd row: P2, [k4, p1] 3 times, k4, p2.

3rd row: K1, yf, k1, p2, p2tog, [k1, p4] twice, k1, p2tog, p2, k1, yf, k1.

4th row: P3, k2, p2, k4, p1, k4, p2, k2, p3.

5th row: K2, yf, k1, p3, k1, p2, p2tog, k1, p2tog, p2, k1, p3, k1, yf, k2.

6th row: P4, k3, p1, k2, p3, k2, p1, k3, p4.

7th row: K3, yf, k1, p1, p2tog, [k1, p3] twice, k1, p2tog, p1, k1, yf, k3.

8th row: P5, k1, p2, k3, p1, k3, p2, k1, p5.

9th row: K4, yf, k1, p2, k1, p1, p2tog, k1, p2tog, p1, k1, p2, k1, yf, k4.

10th row: P6, k2, p1, k1, p3, k1, p1, k2, p6.

11th row: K5, yf, k1, p2tog, [k1, p2] twice, k1, p2tog, k1, yf, k5.

12th row: P9, k2, p1, k2, p9.

13th row: K6, yf, k1, p1, k1, [p2tog, k1] twice, p1, k1, yf, k6.

14th row: P8, k1, p5, k1, p8.

Rep these 14 rows.

Corona Pattern Stitch

Multiple of 10 + 1.

1st row (right side): K3, k2tog, yf, k1, yf, sl 1, k1, psso, *k5, k2tog, yf, k1, yf, sl 1, k1, psso; rep from * to last 3 sts, k3.

2nd, 4th, 6th, and 8th rows: Purl.

3rd row: K2, k2tog, yf, k3, yf, sl 1, k1, psso, *k3, k2tog, yf, k3, yf, sl 1, k1, psso; rep from * to last 2 sts, k2.

5th row: K1, *k2tog, yf, k5, yf, sl 1, k1, psso, k1; rep from * to end.

7th row: Knit.

9th row: K6, *insert right-hand needle in first space of 5th row, yrn and draw through to make a long loop which is kept on needle; rep from * into each of remaining 5 spaces of leaf from right to left, k10; rep from * to last 5 sts, take up a long loop as before in next 6 spaces, knit to end.

10th row: P5, purl tog the 6 long loops with the next st, *p9, purl tog the 6 long loops with the next st; rep from * to last 5 sts, p5.

11th row: Knit.

12th, 14th, 16th, 18th, and 20th rows: Purl.

13th row: K1, *yf, sl 1, k1, psso, k5, k2tog, yf, k1; rep from * to end.

15th row: K2, yf, sl 1, k1, psso, k3, k2tog, yf, *k3, yf, sl 1, k1, psso, k3, k2tog, yf; rep from * to last 2 sts, k2.

17th row: K3, yf, sl 1, k1, psso, k1, k2tog, yf, *k5, yf, sl 1, k1, psso, k1, k2tog, yf; rep from * to last 3 sts, k3.

19th row: Knit.

21st row: K1, take up a long loop as before in next 3 spaces, k10, *take up a long loop in each of next 6 spaces, k10; rep from * to last st, take up a long loop in each of next 3 spaces.

22nd row: Purl tog the first 3 long loops with the next st, p9, *purl tog the 6 long loops with the next st, p9; rep from * to last st, purl tog the last 3 long loops with the last st.

23rd row: Knit.

24th row: Purl.

Rep these 24 rows.

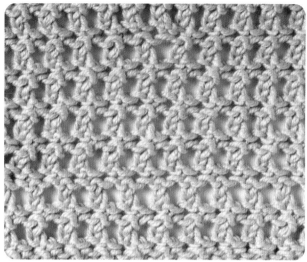

King Charles Brocade

Worked over 11 sts on a background of St st.

1st row (right side): P2, k2tog, [k1, yf] twice, k1, sl 1, k1, psso, p2.

2nd and every alt row: K2, p7, k2.

3rd row: P2, k2tog, yf, k3, yf, sl 1, k1, psso, p2.

5th row: P2, k1, yf, sl 1, k1, psso, k1, k2tog, yf, k1, p2.

7th row: P2, k2, yf, sl 1, k2tog, psso, yf, k2, p2.

8th row: As 2nd row.

Rep these 8 rows.

Ridge and Hole Pattern

Multiple of 2 + 1.

Note: Sts should only be counted after the 1st, 3rd or 4th rows of this pattern.

1st row (right side): Purl.

2nd row: *P2tog; rep from * to last st, p1.

3rd row: P1, *purl through horizontal strand of yarn lying between stitch just worked and next st, p1; rep from * to end.

4th row: P1, *yrn, p2tog; rep from * to end.

Rep these 4 rows.

Arched Windows

Worked over 13 sts on a background of reverse St st.

Note: Sts should not be counted after the 3rd, 4th, 7th or 8th rows.

T5R (Twist 5 Right) = slip next 3 sts onto cable needle and hold at back of work, knit next 2 sts from left-hand needle, then p1, k2 from cable needle.

1st row (right side): K2, p2, k2tog, yf, k1, yf, sl 1, k1, psso, p2, k2.

2nd row: P2, k2, p5, k2, p2.

3rd row: K2, p2, k1, yf, k3, yf, k1, p2, k2.

4th row: P2, k2, p7, k2, p2.

5th row: K2, p2, yb, sl 1, k1, psso, yf, sl 1, k2tog, psso, yf, k2tog, p2, k2.

6th row: As 2nd row.

7th row: T3F, p1, k1, yf, k3, yf, k1, p1, T3B.

8th row: K1, p2, k1, p7, k1, p2, k1.

9th row: P1, T3F, sl 1, k1, psso, yf, sl 1, k2tog, psso, yf, k2tog, T3B, p1.

10th row: K2, p9, k2.

11th row: P2, T3F, p3, T3B, p2.

12th row: [K3, p2] twice, k3.

13th row: P3, T3F, p1, T3B, p3.

14th row: K4, p2, k1, p2, k4.

15th row: P4, T5R, p4.

16th row: Knit.

Rep these 16 rows.

Pillar Openwork

Multiple of 3 + 2.

1st row (right side): K1, *yf, sl 1 purlwise, k2, psso the k2;
rep from * to last st, k1.

2nd row: Purl.

Rep these 2 rows.

Ridged Lace

Multiple of 2.

1st row (right side): K1, *yf, K2tog tbl; rep from * to last st, k1.

2nd row: P1, *yrn, p2tog; rep from * to last st, p1.

Rep these 2 rows.

Knitted fabric can be manipulated to produce stunning results. Experiment and discover what type of effects can be created through lace knitting.

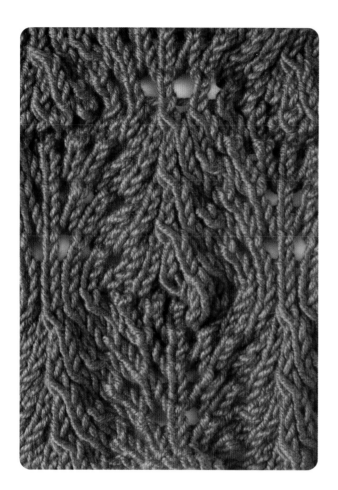

Peacock Plume

Multiple of 16 sts + 1.

1st and 3rd rows (wrong side): Purl.

2nd row: Knit.

4th row: [K1, yf] 3 times, [sl 1, k1, psso] twice, sl 2, k1, p2sso, [k2tog] twice, *yf, [k1, yf] 5 times, [sl 1, k1, psso] twice, sl 2, k1, p2sso, [k2tog] twice; rep from * to last 3 sts, [yf, k1] 3 times.

5th through 16th rows: Rep the last 4 rows 3 times more.

17th and 19th rows: Purl.

18th row: Knit.

20th row: [K2tog] 3 times, [yf, k1] 5 times, *yf, [sl 1, k1, psso] twice, sl 2, k1, p2sso, [k2tog] twice, [yf, k1] 5 times; rep from * to last 6 sts, yf, [sl 1, k1, psso] 3 times.

21st through 32nd rows: Rep the last 4 rows 3 times more.

Rep these 32 rows.

Little Crown

Multiple of 3 + 2.

1st row (right side): Knit.

2nd row: Knit.

3rd row: K1, knit to last st wrapping yarn twice around needle for each st, k1.

4th row: K1, *pass next 3 sts to right-hand needle dropping extra loops, pass these 3 sts back to left-hand needle, k1, p1, k1 through 3 sts tog; rep from * to last st, k1.

Rep these 4 rows.

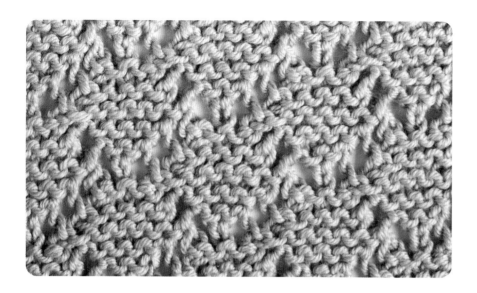

Garter Stitch Lacy Diamonds

Multiple of 10 + 1.

1st and every alt row (right side): Knit.

2nd row: K3, *k2tog, yf, k1, yf, k2tog, k5; rep from * to last 8 sts, k2tog, yf, k1, yf, k2tog, k3.

4th row: K2, *k2tog, yf, k3, yf, k2tog, k3; rep from * to last 9 sts, k2tog, yf, k3, yf, k2tog, k2.

6th row: K1, *k2tog, yf, k5, yf, k2tog, k1; rep from * to end.

8th row: K1, *yf, k2tog, k5, k2tog, yf, k1; rep from * to end.

10th row: K2, *yf, k2tog, k3, k2tog, yf, k3; rep from * to last 9 sts, yf, k2tog, k3, k2tog, yf, k2.

12th row: K3, *yf, k2tog, k1, k2tog, yf, k5; rep from * to last 8 sts, yf, k2tog, k1, k2tog, yf, k3.

Rep these 12 rows.

Leaf Panel

Worked over 24 sts on a background of St st.

1st row (right side): Sl 1, k2tog, psso, k7, yf, k1, yfrn, p2, yon, k1, yf, k7, k3tog.

2nd and every alt row: P11, k2, p11.

3rd row: Sl 1, k2tog, psso, k6, [yf, k1] twice, p2, [k1, yf] twice, k6, k3tog.

5th row: Sl 1, k2tog, psso, k5, yf, k1, yf, k2, p2, k2, yf, k1, yf, k5, k3tog.

7th row: Sl 1, k2tog, psso, k4, yf, k1, yf, k3, p2, k3, yf, k1, yf, k4, k3tog.

9th row: Sl 1, k2tog, psso, k3, yf, k1, yf, k4, p2, k4, yf, k1, yf, k3, k3tog.

10th row: As 2nd row.

Rep these 10 rows.

Twisted Openwork
Pattern 1

Multiple of 4 + 1.

1st row (right side): P1, *k3, p1; rep from * to end.

2nd row: K1, *p3, k1; rep from * to end.

3rd row: As 1st row.

4th row: K1, *yfrn, p3tog, yon, k1; rep from * to end.

5th row: K2, p1, *k3, p1; rep from * to last 2 sts, k2.

6th row: P2, k1, *p3, k1; rep from * to last 2 sts, p2.

7th row: As 5th row.

8th row: P2tog, yon, k1, yfrn, *p3tog, yon, k1, yfrn; rep from * to last 2 sts, p2tog.

Rep these 8 rows.

When knitting a garment as a gift, consider knitting a traditional bottom-to-top design. Should the garment not fit, it will be easier to change the neckline or overall length.

Knotted Boxes I

Multiple of 8 + 5.

1st row (right side): Knit.

2nd row: Purl.

3rd row: K1, p3, *k5, p3; rep from * to last st, k1.

4th row: P1, k3, *p5, k3; rep from * to last st, p1.

5th row: K1, yf, k3tog, yf, *k5, yf, k3tog, yf; rep from * to last st, k1.

Work 3 rows in St st, starting purl.

9th row: K5, *p3, k5; rep from * to end.

10th row: P5, *k3, p5; rep from * to end.

11th row: K5, *yf, k3tog, yf, k5; rep from * to end.

12th row: Purl.

Rep these 12 rows.

Crowns of Glory (Cat's Paw)

Multiple of 14 + 1.

Note: Sts should only be counted after the 7th, 8th, 9th, 10th, 11th and 12th rows.

1st row (right side): K1, *sl 1, k1, psso, k9, k2tog, k1; rep from * to end.

2nd row: P1, *p2tog, p7, p2tog tbl, p1; rep from * to end.

3rd row: K1, *sl 1, k1, psso, k2, [yf] 3 times, k3, k2tog, k1; rep from * to end.

4th row: P1, *p2tog, p2, [k1, p1, k1, p1, k1] into [yf] 3 times making 5 sts, p1, p2tog tbl, p1; rep from * to end.

5th row: K1, *sl 1, k1, psso, k6, k2tog, k1; rep from * to end.

6th row: P1, *p2tog, p7; rep from * to end.

7th row: K2, [yf, k1] 5 times, yf, *k3, [yf, k1] 5 times, yf; rep from * to last 2 sts, k2.

8th row: Purl.

9th and 10th rows: Knit.

11th row: Purl.

12th row: Knit.

Rep these 12 rows.

Fishtail Lace

Multiple of 8 + 1.

1st row (right side): K1, *yf, k2, sl 1, k2tog, psso, k2, yf, k1;
rep from * to end.

2nd row: Purl.

3rd row: K2, *yf, k1, sl 1, k2tog, psso, k1, yf, k3; rep from *
to last 7 sts, yf, k1, sl 1, k2tog, psso, k1, yf, k2.

4th row: Purl.

5th row: K3, *yf, sl 1, k2tog, psso, yf, k5; rep from * to last
6 sts, yf, sl 1, k2tog, psso, yf, k3.

6th row: Purl.

Rep these 6 rows.

Open Diamonds
with Bobbles

Multiple of 10 + 1.

1st row (right side): P1, *yon, sl 1, k1, psso, p5, k2tog, yfrn, p1; rep from * to end.

2nd row: K2, *p1, k5, p1, k3; rep from * to last 9 sts, p1, k5, p1, k2.

3rd row: P2, *yon, sl 1, k1, psso, p3, k2tog, yfrn, p3; rep from * to last 9 sts, yon, sl 1, k1, psso, p3, k2tog, yfrn, p2.

4th row: K3, *p1, k3, p1, k5; rep from * to last 8 sts, p1, k3, p1, k3.

5th row: P3, *yon, sl 1, k1, psso, p1, k2tog, yfrn, p5; rep from * to last 8 sts, yon, sl 1, k1, psso, p1, k2tog, yfrn, p3.

6th row: K4, *p1, k1, p1, k7; rep from * to last 7 sts, p1, k1, p1, k4.

7th row: P4, *yon, sl 1, k2tog, psso, yfrn, p3, make bobble (MB) as follows: [k1, p1, k1, p1, k1] into next st, turn and k5, turn and p5, turn and sl 1, k1, psso, k1, k2tog, turn and p3tog, (bobble completed), p3; rep from * to last 7 sts, yon, sl 1, k2tog, psso, yfrn, p4.

8th row: K4, *p3, k3, PB1, k3; rep from * to last 7 sts, p3, k4.

9th row: P3, *k2tog, yfrn, p1, yon, sl 1, k1, psso, p5; rep from * to last 8 sts, k2tog, yfrn, p1, yon, sl 1, k1, psso, p3.

10th row: K3, *p1, k3, p1, k5; rep from * to last 8 sts, p1, k3, p1, k3.

11th row: P2, *k2tog, yfrn, p3, yon, sl 1, k1, psso, p3; rep from * to last 9 sts, k2tog, yfrn, p3, yon, sl 1, k1, psso, p2.

12th row: K2, *p1, k5, p1, k3; rep from * to last 9 sts, p1, k5, p1, k2.

13th row: P1, *k2tog, yfrn, p5, yon, sl 1, k1, psso, p1; rep from * to end.

14th row: K1, *p1, k7, p1, k1; rep from * to end.

15th row: K2tog, *yfrn, p3, MB, p3, yon, sl 1, k2tog, psso; rep from * to last 9 sts, yfrn p3, MB, p3, yon, sl 1, k1, psso.

16th row: P2, *k3, PB1, k3, p3; rep from * to last 9 sts, k3, PB1, k3, p2.

Rep these 16 rows.

Fishtail Lace Panel

Worked over 11 sts on a background of St st.

1st row (right side): P1, k1, yf, k2, sl 1, k2tog, psso, k2, yf, k1, p1.

2nd row: K1, p9, k1.

3rd row: P1, k2, yf, k1, sl 1, k2tog, psso, k1, yf, k2, p1.

4th row: As 2nd row.

5th row: P1, k3, yf, sl 1, k2tog, psso, yf, k3, p1.

6th row: As 2nd row.

Rep these 6 rows.

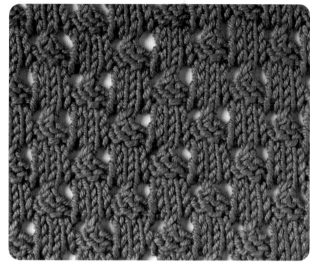

Twisted Openwork Pattern II

Work as Twisted Openwork Pattern I on page 90, using reverse side as right side.

Knotted Boxes II

Multiple of 6 + 5.

1st row (right side): K1, p3, *k3, p3; rep from * to last st, k1.

2nd row: P1, k3, *p3, k3; rep from * to last st, p1.

3rd row: K1, yf, k3tog, yf, *k3, yf, k3tog, yf; rep from * to last st, k1.

4th row: Purl.

5th row: K4, p3, *k3, p3; rep from * to last 4 sts, k4.

6th row: P4, k3, *p3, k3; rep from * to last 4 sts, p4.

7th row: K4, yf, k3tog, yf, *k3, yf, k3tog, yf; rep from * to last 4 sts, k4.

8th row: Purl.

Rep these 8 rows.

Bobble Spray Panel

Worked over 23 sts on a background of reverse St st.

1st row (right side): Sl 1, k1, psso, k6, [yf, k1] twice, sl 1, k2tog, psso, [k1, yf] twice, k6, k2tog.

2nd and every alt row: Purl.

3rd row: Sl 1, k1, psso, k5, yf, k1, yf, k2, sl 1, k2tog, psso, k2, yf, k1, yf, k5, k2tog.

5th row: Sl 1, k1, psso, k4, yf, k1, yf, MB, k2, sl 1, k2tog, psso, k2, MB, yf, k1, yf, k4, k2tog.

7th row: Sl 1, k1, psso, k3, yf, k1, yf, MB, k3, sl 1, k2tog, psso, k3, MB, yf, k1, yf, k3, k2tog.

9th row: Sl 1, k1, psso, k2, yf, k1, yf, MB, k4, sl 1, k2tog, psso, k4, MB, yf, k1, yf, k2, k2tog.

11th row: Sl 1, k1, psso, [k1, yf] twice, MB, k5, sl 1, k2tog, psso, k5, MB, [yf, k1] twice, k2tog.

13th row: Sl 1, k1, psso, yf, k1, yf, MB, k6, sl 1, k2tog, psso, k6, MB, yf, k1, yf, k2tog.

14th row: Purl.

Rep these 14 rows.

Herringbone Lace Rib

Multiple of 7 + 1.

1st row (right side): K1, *p1, k1, yfrn, p2tog, k1, p1, k1; rep from * to end.

2nd row: P1, *k2, yfrn, p2tog, k2, p1; rep from * to end.

Rep these 2 rows.

Lace is not as daunting as it may appear; after all, it is simply comprised of increases and decreases.

Vandyke Lace Panel I

Worked over 17 sts on a background of St st.

1st row (right side): *K2tog, yf, k1, yf, sl 1, k1, psso*, k3, yf,
sl 1, k1, psso, k2, rep from * to * once more.

2nd row: Purl.

3rd row: [K2tog, yf, k1, yf, sl 1, k1, psso, k1] twice, k2tog, yf,
k1, yf, sl 1, k1, psso.

4th row: Purl.

5th row: *K2tog, yf, k1, yf, sl 1, k1, psso*, k2tog, yf, k3, yf,
sl 1, k1, psso, rep from * to * once more.

6th row: Purl.

Rep these 6 rows.

Ornamental Tulip Pattern

Multiple of 13.

Note: Sts should only be counted after the 1st, 2nd, 9th and 10th rows of this pattern.

1st row (right side): Purl.

2nd row: Knit.

3rd row: P6, [p1, k1] 3 times into next st, *p12, [p1, k1] 3 times into next st; rep from * to last 6 sts, p6.

4th row: K6, p6, *k12, p6; rep from * to last 6 sts, k6.

5th row: P6, k6, *p12, k6; rep from * to last 6 sts, p6.

6th row: As 4th row.

7th row: [P2tog] twice, p2, [k2, yf] twice, k2, *p2, [p2tog] 4 times, p2, [k2, yf] twice, k2; rep from * to last 6 sts, p2, [p2tog] twice.

8th row: K4, p8, *k8, p8; rep from * to last 4 sts, k4.

9th row: [P2tog] twice, [k2tog, yf, k1, yf] twice, k2tog, *[p2tog] 4 times, [k2tog, yf, k1, yf] twice, k2tog; rep from * to last 4 sts, [p2tog] twice.

10th row: K2, p9, *k4, p9; rep from * to last 2 sts, k2.

Rep these 10 rows.

Vandyke Lace Panel II

Worked over 9 sts on a background of St st.

1st row (right side): K4, yf, sl 1, k1, psso, k3.

2nd and every alt row: Purl.

3rd row: K2, k2tog, yf, k1, yf, sl 1, k1, psso, k2.

5th row: K1, k2tog, yf, k3, yf, sl 1, k1, psso, k1.

7th row: K2tog, yf, k5, yf, sl 1, k1, psso.

8th row: Purl.

Rep these 8 rows.

Eyelet V-Stitch

Multiple of 12 + 1.

1st row (right side): Knit.

2nd and every alt row: Purl.

3rd row: K4, yf, sl 1, k1, psso, k1, k2tog, yf, *k7, yf, sl 1, k1, psso, k1, k2tog, yf; rep from * to last 4 sts, k4.

5th row: K5, yf, sl 1, k2tog, psso, yf, *k9, yf, sl 1, k2tog, psso, yf; rep from * to last 5 sts, k5.

7th row: Knit.

9th row: K1, *k2tog, yf, k7, yf, sl 1, k1, psso, k1; rep from * to end.

11th row: K2tog, yf, k9, *yf, sl 1, k2tog, psso, yf, k9; rep from * to last 2 sts, yf, sl 1, k1, psso.

12th row: Purl.

Rep these 12 rows.

Diamond Lace I

Multiple of 8 + 7.

1st row (right side): Knit.

2nd row and every alt row: Purl.

3rd row: K3, *yf, sl 1, k1, psso, k6; rep from * to last 4 sts, yf, sl 1, k1, psso, k2.

5th row: K2, *yf, sl 1, k2tog, psso, yf, k5; rep from * to last 5 sts, yf, sl 1, k2tog, psso, yf, k2.

7th row: As 3rd row.

9th row: Knit.

11th row: K7, *yf, sl 1, k1, psso, k6; rep from * to end.

13th row: K6, *yf, sl 1, k2tog, psso, yf, k5; rep from * to last st, k1.

15th row: As 11th row.

16th row: Purl.

Rep these 16 rows.

Canterbury Bells

Multiple of 5.

Note: Sts should only be counted after the 1st, 2nd and 10th rows.

1st row (right side): P2, KB1, *p4, KB1; rep from * to last 2 sts, p2.

2nd row: K2, PB1, *k4, PB1; rep from * to last 2 sts, k2.

3rd row: P2, KB1, *p2, turn, cast on 8 sts cable method, turn, p2, KB1; rep from * to last 2 sts, p2.

4th row: K2, PB1, *k2, p8, k2, PB1; rep from * to last 2 sts, k2.

5th row: P2, KB1, *p2, k8, p2, KB1; rep from * to last 2 sts, p2.

6th row: As 4th row.

7th row: P2, KB1, *p2, yb, sl 1, k1, psso, k4, k2tog, p2, KB1; rep from * to last 2 sts, p2.

8th row: K2, PB1, *k2, p2tog, p2, p2tog tbl, k2, PB1; rep from * to last 2 sts, k2.

9th row: P2, KB1, *p2, yb, sl 1, k1, psso, k2tog, p2, KB1; rep from * to last 2 sts, p2.

10th row: K2, PB1, *k1, sl 1, k1, psso, k2tog, k1, PB1; rep from * to last 2 sts, k2.

Rep these 10 rows.

Ridged Lace Pattern

Multiple of 2 + 1.

Purl 3 rows.

4th row (right side): K1, *yf, sl 1, k1, psso; rep from * to end.

Purl 3 rows.

8th row: K1, *yf, k2tog; rep from * to end.

Rep these 8 rows.

A yarnover is the most common increase in lace patterns. The increase is made by wrapping the yarn once around the RH needle, but without doing any stitches with the LH needle. It's one of the easiest increases out there!

Lace and Cable Pattern

Worked over 21 sts on a St st background.

Special Abbreviation: CB4F or CB4B (Cable-Back 4 Front or Back) = slip next 2 sts onto a cable needle and hold at front (or back) of work, knit into the back of next 2 sts on left-hand needle, then knit into the back of sts on cable needle.

1st row (right side): P2, [KB1] 4 times, k1, yf, k2tog tbl, k3, k2tog, yf, k1, [KB1] 4 times, p2.

2nd and every alt row: K2, [PB1] 4 times, k1, p7, k1, [PB1] 4 times, k2.

3rd row: P2, [KB1] 4 times, k2, yf, k2tog tbl, k1, k2tog, yf, k2, [KB1] 4 times, p2.

5th row: P2, CB4F (see Special Abbreviation), k3, yf, sl 1, k2tog, psso, yf, k3, CB4B, p2.

7th row: P2, [KB1] 4 times, k9, [KB1] 4 times, p2.

8th row: As 2nd row.

Rep these 8 rows.

Pine Cone Pattern

Multiple of 10 + 1.

1st row (right side): Knit.

2nd and every alt row: Purl.

3rd row: K3, k2tog, yf, k1, yf, sl 1, k1, psso, *k5, k2tog, yf, k1, yf, sl 1, k1, psso; rep from * to last 3 sts, k3.

5th row: K2, k2tog, yf, k3, yf, sl 1, k1, psso, *k3, k2tog, yf, k3, yf, sl 1, k1, psso; rep from * to last 2 sts, k2.

7th and 9th rows: As 3rd row.

11th row: Knit.

13th row: K1, *yf, sl 1, k1, psso, k5, k2tog, yf, k1; rep from * to end.

15th row: K2, yf, sl 1, k1, psso, k3, k2tog, yf, *k3, yf, sl 1, k1, psso, k3, k2tog, yf; rep from * to last 2 sts, k2.

17th and 19th rows: As 13th row.

20th row: Purl.

Rep these 20 rows.

Imitation Crochet

Multiple of 6 + 3.

Note: Sts should not be counted after the 1st and 5th row.

1st row (wrong side): K1, *yf, k1; rep from * to end.

2nd row: Knit, dropping yfs off previous row.

3rd row: K1, k3tog, *[yfon] twice (2 sts made), k1, [yfon] twice, sl 2, k3tog, pass both sl sts over; rep from * to last 5 sts, [yfon] twice, k1, [yfon] twice, k3tog, k1.

4th row: K2, *k into front of first loop and back of 2nd loop of double yfon of previous row, k1; rep from * to last st, k1.

5th row: As 1st row.

6th row: As 2nd row.

7th row: K2, *[yfon] twice, sl 2, k3tog, pass both sl sts over, [yfon] twice, k1; rep from * to last st, k1.

8th row: As 4th row.

Rep these 8 rows.

Hyacinth Blossom Stitch

Multiple of 6 + 2.

1st row (wrong side): K1, *p5tog, [k1, p1, k1, p1, k1] into next st; rep from * to last st, k1.

2nd row: Purl.

3rd row: K1, *[k1, p1, k1, p1, k1] into next st, p5tog; rep from * to last st, k1.

4th row: As 2nd row.

5th row: Knit this row winding yarn around the needle 3 times for each st.

6th row: Purl to end dropping extra loops.

Rep these 6 rows.

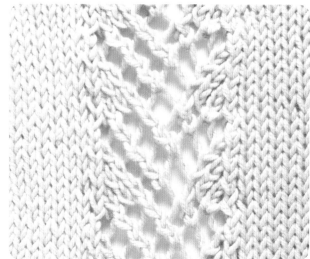

Feather Lace

Multiple of 6 + 1.

1st row (right side): K1, *yf, k2tog tbl, k1, k2tog, yf, k1; rep from * to end.

2nd and every alt row: Purl.

3rd row: K1, *yf, k1, sl 1, k2tog, psso, k1, yf, k1; rep from * to end.

5th row: K1, *k2tog, yf, k1, yf, k2tog tbl, k1; rep from * to end.

7th row: K2tog, *[k1, yf] twice, k1, sl 1, k2tog, psso; rep from * to last 5 sts, [k1, yf] twice, k1, k2tog tbl.

8th row: Purl.

Rep these 8 rows.

Fan Lace Panel

Worked over 11 sts on a background of St st.

1st row (right side): Sl 1, k1, psso, [KB1] 3 times, yf, k1, yf, [KB1] 3 times, k2tog.

2nd and every alt row: Purl.

3rd row: Sl 1, k1, psso, [KB1] twice, yf, k1, yf, sl 1, k1, psso, yf, [KB1] twice, k2tog.

5th row: Sl 1, k1, psso, KB1, yf, k1, [yf, sl 1, k1, psso] twice, yf, KB1, k2tog.

7th row: Sl 1, k1, psso, yf, k1, [yf, sl 1, k1, psso] 3 times, yf, k2tog.

8th row: Purl.

Rep these 8 rows.

Raindrops

Multiple of 6 + 5.

1st row (right side): P5, *yrn, p2tog, p4; rep from * to end.

2nd row: K5, *p1, k5; rep from * to end.

3rd row: P5, *k1, p5; rep from * to end.

Rep the last 2 rows once more, then the 2nd row again.

7th row: P2, yrn, p2tog, *p4, yrn, p2tog; rep from * to last st, p1.

8th row: K2, p1, *k5, p1; rep from * to last 2 sts, k2.

9th row: P2, k1, *p5, k1; rep from * to last 2 sts, p2.

Rep the last 2 rows once more, then the 8th row again.

Rep these 12 rows.

Make it a practice to work with good light.

Mesh Zigzag Stitch

Multiple of 11.

Special Abbreviation: KW5 = knit 5 sts wrapping yarn twice around needle for each st.

1st row (right side): K1, KW5, *k6, KW5; rep from * to last 5 sts, k5.

2nd row: P5, k5 dropping extra loops, *p6, k5 dropping extra loops; rep from * to last st, p1.

3rd row: K2, KW5, *k6, KW5; rep from * to last 4 sts, k4.

4th row: P4, k5 dropping extra loops, *p6, k5 dropping extra loops; rep from * to last 2 sts, p2.

5th row: K3, KW5, *k6, KW5; rep from * to last 3 sts, k3.

6th row: P3, k5 dropping extra loops, *p6, k5 dropping extra loops; rep from * to last 3 sts, p3.

7th row: K4, KW5, *k6, KW5; rep from * to last 2 sts, k2.

8th row: P2, k5 dropping extra loops, *p6, k5 dropping extra loops; rep from * to last 4 sts, p4.

9th row: K5, KW5, *k6, KW5; rep from * to last st, k1.

10th row: P1, k5 dropping extra loops, *p6, k5 dropping extra loops; rep from * to last 5 sts, p5.

11th row: As 7th row.

12th row: As 8th row.

13th row: As 5th row.

14th row: As 6th row.

15th row: As 3rd row.

16th row: As 4th row.

17th row: As 1st row.

18th row: As 2nd row.

Rep these 18 rows.

Arch Lace Panel

Worked over 11 sts on a background of St st.

1st row (right side): K1, yf, k2tog, k5, sl 1, k1, psso, yf, k1.

2nd and every alt row: Purl.

3rd row: As 1st row.

5th row: As 1st row.

7th row: K1, yf, k3, sl 1, k2tog, psso, k3, yf, k1.

9th row: K2, yf, k2, sl 1, k2tog, psso, k2, yf, k2.

11th row: K3, yf, k1, sl 1, k2tog, psso, k1, yf, k3.

13th row: K4, yf, sl 1, k2tog, psso, yf, k4.

14th row: Purl.

Rep these 14 rows.

Lozenge Lace Panel

Worked over 11 sts on a background of St st.

1st row (right side): K1, yf, sl 1, k1, psso, k5, k2tog, yf, k1.

2nd and every alt row: Purl.

3rd row: K2, yf, sl 1, k1, psso, k3, k2tog, yf, k2.

5th row: K3, yf, sl 1, k1, psso, k1, k2tog, yf, k3.

7th row: K4, yf, sl 1, k2tog, psso, yf, k4.

9th row: K3, k2tog, yf, k1, yf, sl 1, k1, psso, k3.

11th row: K2, k2tog, yf, k3, yf, sl 1, k1, psso, k2.

13th row: K1, k2tog, yf, k5, yf, sl 1, k1, psso, k1.

15th row: K2tog, yf, k7, yf, sl 1, k1, psso.

16th row: Purl.

Rep these 16 rows.

Bobble Tree Panel

Worked over 17 sts on a background of reverse St st.

1st row (right side): P6, k2tog, yfrn, p1, yon, sl 1, k1, psso, p6.

2nd row: K6, p1, k3, p1, k6.

3rd row: P5, k2tog, yfrn, p3, yon, sl 1, k1, psso, p5.

4th row: [K5, p1] twice, k5.

5th row: P4, k2tog, yfrn, [p1, k1] twice, p1, yon, sl 1, k1, psso, p4.

6th row: K4, p1, k2, p1, k1, p1, k2, p1, k4.

7th row: P3, k2tog, yfrn, p2, k1, p1, k1, p2, yon, sl 1, k1, psso, p3.

8th row: [K3, p1] twice, k1, [p1, k3] twice.

9th row: P2, k2tog, yfrn, p2, k2tog, yfrn, p1, yon, sl 1, k1, psso, p2, yon, sl 1, k1, psso, p2.

10th row: K2, [p1, k3] 3 times, p1, k2.

11th row: P2, [k1, p1] twice into next st, turn and p4, turn and k4, turn and p4, turn and sl 1, k1, psso, k2tog, turn and p2tog, turn and slip bobble st onto right-hand needle (bobble completed), p2, k2tog, yfrn, p3, yon, sl 1, k1, psso, p2, make bobble, p2.

12th row: [K5, p1] twice, k5.

Rep these 12 rows.

Snowflakes 1

Multiple of 8 + 7.

1st and every alt row (wrong side): Purl.

2nd row: K5, sl 1, k1, psso, yf, k1, yf, k2tog, *k3, sl 1, k1, psso, yf, k1, yf, k2tog; rep from * to last 5 sts, k5.

4th row: K6, yf, sl 2, k1, p2sso, yf, *k5, yf, sl 2, k1, p2sso, yf; rep from * to last 6 sts, k6.

6th row: As 2nd row.

8th row: K1, sl 1, k1, psso, yf, k1, yf, k2tog, *k3, sl 1, k1, psso, yf, k1, yf, k2tog; rep from * to last st, k1.

10th row: K2, yf, sl 2, k1, p2sso, yf, *k5, yf, sl 2, k1, p2sso, yf; rep from * to last 2 sts, k2.

12th row: As 8th row.

Rep these 12 rows.

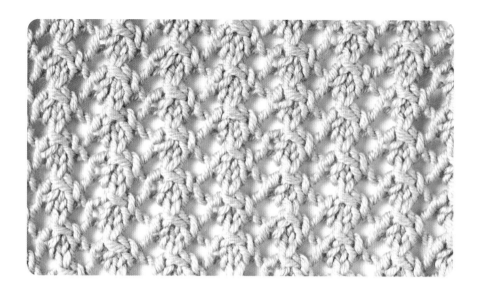

Trellis Lace

Multiple of 6 + 5.

1st row (right side): K4, *yf, sl 1, k2tog, psso, yf, k3; rep from * to last st, k1.

2nd row: Purl.

3rd row: K1, *yf, sl 1, k2tog, psso, yf, k3; rep from * to last 4 sts, yf, sl 1, k2tog, psso, yf, k1.

4th row: Purl.

Rep these 4 rows.

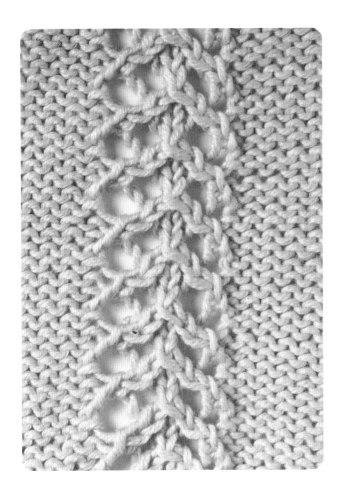

Lace Rib Panel

Worked over 7 sts on a background of reverse St st.

1st row (right side): P1, yon, sl 1, k1, psso, k1, k2tog, yfrn, p1.

2nd row: K1, p5, k1.

3rd row: P1, k1, yf, sl 1, k2tog, psso, yf, k1, p1.

4th row: K1, p5, k1.

Rep these 4 rows.

The foundation to knitted lace is to balance the relationship between increases and decreases.

Quatrefoil Panel

Worked over 15 sts on a background of St st.

Note: Sts should not be counted after the 6th, 7th, 8th or 9th rows.

1st row (right side): K5, k2tog, yf, k1, yf, sl 1, k1, psso, k5.

2nd row: P4, p2tog tbl, yrn, p3, yrn, p2tog, p4.

3rd row: K3, k2tog, yf, k5, yf, sl 1, k1, psso, k3.

4th row: P2, p2tog tbl, yrn, p1, yrn, p2tog, p1, p2tog tbl, yrn, p1, yrn, p2tog, p2.

5th row: K1, k2tog, yf, k3, yf, k3tog, yf, k3, yf, sl 1, k1, psso, k1.

6th row: P2, yrn, p5, yrn, p1, yrn, p5, yrn, p2.

7th row: [K3, yf, sl 1, k1, psso, k1, k2tog, yf] twice, k3.

8th row: P4, p3tog, yrn, p5, yrn, p3tog, p4.

9th row: K6, yf, sl 1, k1, psso, k1, k2tog, yf, k6.

10th row: P3, p2tog tbl, p2, yrn, p3tog, yrn, p2, p2tog, p3.

Rep these 10 rows.

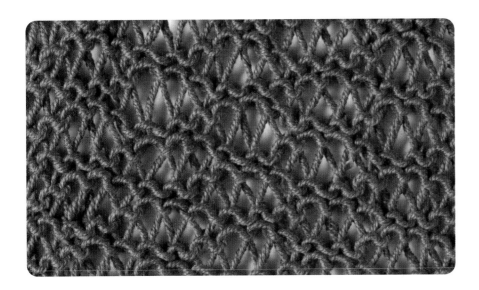

Wave Stitch

Multiple of 6 + 1.

Special Abbreviations: KW2 = knit next st wrapping yarn twice around needle.

KW3 = knit next st wrapping yarn 3 times around needle.

1st row (right side): K1, *KW2, [KW3] twice, KW2, k2; rep from * to end.

2nd row: Knit dropping all extra loops of previous row.

3rd row: KW3, KW2, k2, KW2, *[KW3] twice, KW2, k2, KW2; rep from * to last 2 sts, KW3, k1.

4th row: As 2nd row.

Rep these 4 rows.

Diamond and Eyelet Pattern

Multiple of 6 + 3.

1st row (wrong side): Knit.

2nd row: P1, *yrn, p2tog; rep from * to end.

3rd and 4th rows: Knit.

5th row and every WS row to 15th row: Purl.

6th row: *K4, yf, sl 1, k1, psso; rep from * to last 3 sts, k3.

8th row: K2, *k2tog, yf, k1, yf, sl 1, k1, psso, k1; rep from * to last st, k1.

10th row: K1, k2tog, yf, *k3, yf, sl 1, k2tog, psso, yf; rep from * to last 6 sts, k3, yf, sl 1, k1, psso, k1.

12th row: K3, *yf, sl 1, k2tog, psso, yf, k3; rep from * to end.

14th row: As 6th row.

16th row: Knit.

Rep these 16 rows.

Snowflakes II

Multiple of 6 + 1.

Note: Sts should not be counted after 3rd, 4th, 9th, and 10th rows.

1st row (right side): K1, *yf, sl 1, k1, psso, k1, k2tog, yf, k1; rep from * to end.

2nd and every alt row: Purl.

3rd row: K2, yf, *k3, yf; rep from * to last 2 sts, k2.

5th row: K2tog, yf, sl 1, k1, psso, k1, k2tog, yf, *sl 1, k2tog, psso, yf, sl 1, k1, psso, k1, k2tog, yf; rep from * to last 2 sts, sl 1, k1, psso.

7th row: K1, *k2tog, yf, k1, yf, sl 1, k1, psso, k1; rep from * to end.

9th row: As 3rd row.

11th row: K1, *k2tog, yf, sl 1, k2tog, psso, yf, sl 1, k1, psso, k1; rep from * to end.

12th row: Purl.

Rep these 12 rows.

Lace Chain Panel

Worked over 10 sts on a background of St st.

1st row (right side): K2, k2tog, yf, k2tog but do not slip from needle, knit the first of these 2 sts again, then slip both sts from needle together, yf, sl 1, k1, psso, k2.

2nd row: Purl.

3rd row: K1, k2tog, yf, k4, yf, sl 1, k1, psso, k1.

4th row: Purl.

5th row: K2tog, yf, k1, k2tog, [yf] twice, sl 1, k1, psso, k1, yf, sl 1, k1, psso.

6th row: P4, k1 into first yf, p1 into 2nd yf, p4.

7th row: K2, yf, sl 1, k1, psso, k2, k2tog, yf, k2.

8th row: Purl.

9th row: K3, yf, sl 1, k1, psso, k2tog, yf, k3.

10th row: Purl.

Rep these 10 rows.

Zigzag Eyelets

Multiple of 9.

1st row (right side): K4, *yf, sl 1, k1, psso, k7; rep from * to last 5 sts, yf, sl 1, k1, psso, k3.

2nd and every alt row: Purl.

3rd row: K5, *yf, sl 1, k1, psso, k7; rep from * to last 4 sts, yf, sl 1, k1, psso, k2.

5th row: K6, *yf, sl 1, k1, psso, k7; rep from * to last 3 sts, yf, sl 1, k1, psso, k1.

7th row: *K7, yf, sl 1, k1, psso; rep from * to end.

9th row: K3, *k2tog, yf, k7; rep from * to last 6 sts, k2tog, yf, k4.

11th row: K2, *k2tog, yf, k7; rep from * to last 7 sts, k2tog, yf, k5.

13th row: K1, *k2tog, yf, k7; rep from * to last 8 sts, k2tog, yf, k6.

15th row: *K2tog, yf, k7; rep from * to end.

16th row: Purl.

Rep these 16 rows.

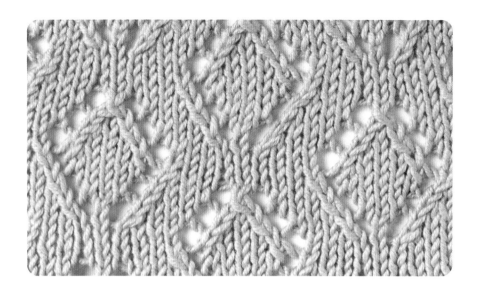

Eyelet Diamonds

Multiple of 16 + 11.

1st row (right side): K10, yf, sl 1, k1, psso, k3, k2tog, yf, *k9, yf, sl 1, k1, psso, k3, k2tog, yf; rep from * to last 10 sts, k10.

2nd and every alt row: Purl.

3rd row: K3, k2tog, yf, k1, yf, sl 1, k1, psso, *k3, yf, sl 1, k1, psso, k1, k2tog, yf, k3, k2tog, yf, k1, yf, sl 1, k1, psso; rep from * to last 3 sts, k3.

5th row: K2, k2tog, yf, k3, yf, sl 1, k1, psso, *k3, yf, sl 1, k2tog, psso, yf, k3, k2tog, yf, k3, yf, sl 1, k1, psso; rep from * to last 2 sts, k2.

7th row: K1, k2tog, yf, k5, yf, sl 1, k1, psso, *k7, k2tog, yf, k5, yf, sl 1, k1, psso; rep from * to last st, k1.

9th row: K2, yf, sl 1, k1, psso, k3, k2tog, yf, *k9, yf, sl 1, k1, psso, k3, k2tog, yf; rep from * to last 2 sts, k2.

11th row: K3, yf, sl 1, k1, psso, k1, k2tog, yf, k3, *k2tog, yf, k1, yf, sl 1, k1, psso, k3, yf, sl 1, k1, psso, k1, k2tog, yf, k3; rep from * to end.

13th row: K4, yf, sl 1, k2tog, psso, yf, *k3, k2tog, yf, k3, yf, sl 1, k1, psso, k3, yf, sl 1, k2tog, psso, yf; rep from * to last 4 sts, k4.

15th row: K9, k2tog, yf, k5, yf, sl 1, k1, psso, *k7, k2tog, yf, k5, yf, sl 1, k1, psso; rep from * to last 9 sts, k9.

16th row: Purl.

Rep these 16 rows.

Lacy Checks

Multiple of 6 + 5.

1st row (right side): K1, *yf, sl 1, k2tog, psso, yf, k3; rep from * to last 4 sts, yf, sl 1, k2tog, psso, yf, k1.

2nd and every alt row: Purl.

3rd row: As 1st row.

5th row: Knit.

7th row: K4, *yf, sl 1, k2tog, psso, yf, k3; rep from * to last st, k1.

9th row: As 7th row.

11th row: Knit.

12th row: Purl.

Rep these 12 rows.

Lace requires stretching to look its best. Avoid inflexible cast-on and cast-off edges.

Openweave Panel

Worked over 11 sts on a background of St st.

1st row (right side): P2, yb, sl 1, k1, psso, yf, k3, yf, k2tog, p2.

2nd row: K2, p7, k2.

3rd row: P2, k2, yf, sl 1, k2tog, psso, yf, k2, p2.

4th row: K2, p7, k2.

Rep these 4 rows.

Double Lace Rib

Multiple of 6 + 2.

1st row (right side): K2, *p1, yon, k2tog tb1, p1, k2; rep from * to end.

2nd row: P2, *k1, p2; rep from * to end.

3rd row: K2, *p1, k2tog, yfrn, p1, k2; rep from * to end.

4th row: As 2nd row.

Rep these 4 rows.

Catherine Wheels

Worked over 13 sts on a background of St st.

Special Abbreviations: Inc 1 (Increase 1) = knit into front and back of next st.

Inc 2 (Increase 2) = knit into front, back and front of next st.

Work 5tog = sl 1, k1, psso, k3tog, pass the st resulting from sl 1, k1, psso over the st resulting from k3tog.

1st and every alt row (wrong side): Purl.

2nd row: K5, sl 3, yf, pass same slipped sts back to left-hand needle, yb, knit 3 slipped sts, k5.

4th row: K3, k3tog, yf, Inc 2, yf, k3tog tbl, k3.

6th row: K1, k3tog, yf, k2tog, yf, Inc 2, yf, sl 1, k1, psso, yf, k3tog tbl, k1.

8th row: [K2tog, yf] 3 times, KB1, [yf, sl 1, k1, psso] 3 times.

10th row: K1, [yf, k2tog] twice, yf, sl 1, k2tog, psso, [yf, sl 1, k1, psso] twice, yf, k1.

12th row: [Sl 1, k1, psso, yf] 3 times, KB1, [yf, k2tog] 3 times.

14th row: K1, Inc 1, yf, sl 1, k1, psso, yf, Work 5tog, yf, k2tog, yf, Inc 1, k1.

16th row: K3, Inc 1, yf, Work 5tog, yf, Inc 1, k3.

Rep these 16 rows.

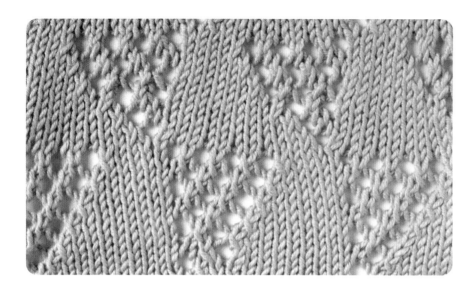

Swinging Triangles

Multiple of 12 + 1.

1st and every alt row (wrong side): Purl.

2nd row: *K10, sl 1, k1, psso, yf; rep from * to last st, k1.

4th row: K9, sl 1, k1, psso, yf, *k10, sl 1, k1, psso, yf; rep from * to last 2 sts, k2.

6th row: *K8, [sl 1, k1, psso, yf] twice; rep from * to last st, k1.

8th row: K7, [sl 1, k1, psso, yf] twice, *k8, [sl 1, k1, psso, yf] twice; rep from * to last 2 sts, k2.

10th row: *K6, [sl 1, k1, psso, yf] 3 times; rep from * to last st, k1.

12th row: K5, [sl 1, k1, psso, yf] 3 times, *k6, [sl 1, k1, psso, yf] 3 times; rep from * to last 2 sts, k2.

14th row: *K4, [sl 1, k1, psso, yf] 4 times; rep from * to last st, k1.

16th row: K1, *yf, k2tog, k10; rep from * to end.

18th row: K2, yf, k2tog, *k10, yf, k2tog; rep from * to last 9 sts, k9.

20th row: K1, *[yf, k2tog] twice, k8; rep from * to end.

22nd row: K2, [yf, k2tog] twice, *k8, [yf, k2tog] twice; rep from * to last 7 sts, k7.

24th row: K1, *[yf, k2tog] 3 times, k6; rep from * to end.

26th row: K2, [yf, k2tog] 3 times, *k6, [yf, k2tog] 3 times; rep from * to last 5 sts, k5.

28th row: K1, *[yf, k2tog] 4 times, k4; rep from * to end.
Rep these 28 rows.

All-Over Eyelets

Multiple of 10 + 1.

1st row (right side): Knit.

2nd and every alt row: Purl.

3rd row: K3, *k2tog, yf, k1, yf, sl 1, k1, psso, k5; rep from * to last 8 sts, k2tog, yf, k1, yf, sl 1, k1, psso, k3.

5th row: Knit.

7th row: K1, *yf, sl 1, k1, psso, k5, k2tog, yf, k1; rep from * to end.

8th row: Purl.

Rep these 8 rows.

Little Lace Panel

Worked over 5 sts on a background of St st.

Note: Sts should not be counted after the 1st or 2nd rows of this pattern.

1st row (right side): K1, yf, k3, yf, k1.

2nd row: Purl.

3rd row: K2, sl 1, k2tog, psso, k2.

4th row: Purl.

Rep these 4 rows.

Eyelet Lace

Multiple of 6 + 2.

Note: Sts should only be counted after the 2nd and 4th row.

1st row (right side): K1, yf, *k2tog tbl, k2, k2tog, yf; rep from * to last st, k1.

2nd row: K1, p5, *p into front and back of next st, p4; rep from * to last 2 sts, p1, k1.

3rd row: K2, *k2tog, yf, k2tog tbl, k2; rep from * to end.

4th row: K1, p2, *p into front and back of next st, p4; rep from * to last 4 sts, p into front and back of next st, p2, k1.

Rep these 4 rows.

Fishtails

Worked over 15 sts on a background of St st.

1st row (right side): K6, yf, sl 1, k2tog, psso, yf, k6.

2nd and every alt row: Purl.

Rep these 2 rows 3 times more.

9th row: [K1, yf] twice, sl 1, k1, psso, k2, sl 1, k2tog, psso, k2, k2tog, [yf, k1] twice.

11th row: K2, yf, k1, yf, sl 1, k1, psso, k1, sl 1, k2tog, psso, k1, k2tog, yf, k1, yf, k2.

13th row: K3, yf, k1, yf, sl 1, k1, psso, sl 1, k2tog, psso, k2tog, yf, k1, yf, k3.

15th row: K4, yf, sl 1, k1, psso, yf, sl 1, k2tog, psso, yf, k2tog, yf, k4.

16th row: Purl.

Rep these 16 rows.

When working with slippery fabrics such as silk, use wooden, bamboo, or coated metal needles to ease the process.

Zigzag Eyelet Panel

Worked over 11 sts on a background of St st.

1st row (right side): K6, yf, sl 1, k1, psso, k3.

2nd and every alt row: Purl.

3rd row: K7, yf, sl 1, k1, psso, k2.

5th row: K3, k2tog, yf, k3, yf, sl 1, k1, psso, k1.

7th row: K2, k2tog, yf, k5, yf, sl 1, k1, psso.

9th row: K1, k2tog, yf, k8.

11th row: K2tog, yf, k9.

12th row: Purl.

Rep these 12 rows.

Snake Panel

Worked over 22 sts on a background of St st.

Special Abbreviations: Work 5tog = sl 1, k1, psso, k3tog, pass the st resulting from sl 1, k1, psso over the st resulting from k3tog.

Inc 1 (Increase 1) = knit into front and back of next st.

Inc 2 (Increase 2) = knit into front, back and front of next st.

Cluster 3 = sl 3, yf, slip same 3 sts back to left-hand needle, yb, k3.

1st row (right side): [K2tog, yf] 3 times, k3, [yf, sl 1, k1, psso] twice, yf, sl 1, k2tog, psso, yf, [k2tog, yf] twice, k2.

2nd and every alt row: Purl.

3rd row: K1, yf, k2tog, yf, sl 2, k1, p2sso, yf, k3, Inc 1, yf, sl 1, k1, psso, yf, Work 5tog, yf, k2tog, yf, Inc 1, k2.

5th row: K1, yf, sl 2, k1, p2sso, yf, sl 1, k1, psso, yf, k5, Inc 1, yf, Work 5tog, yf, Inc 1, k4.

7th row: K1, yf, k2tog, yf, sl 2, k1, p2sso, yf, k7, Cluster 3, k6.

9th row: K1, yf, sl 2, k1, p2sso, yf, sl 1, k1, psso, yf, k5, k3tog, yf, Inc 2, yf, k3tog tbl, k4.

11th row: K1, yf, k2tog, yf, sl 2, k1, p2sso, yf, k3, k3tog, yf, k2tog, yf, Inc 2, yf, sl 1, k1, psso, yf, k3tog tbl, k2.

13th row: K1, yf, sl 2, k1, p2sso, yf, sl 1, k1, psso, yf, k2, [k2tog, yf] 3 times, k1, [yf, sl 1, k1, psso] 3 times, k1.

15th row: K2, [yf, sl 1, k1, psso] twice, yf, sl 1, k2tog, psso, yf, [k2tog, yf] twice, k3, [yf, sl 1, k1, psso] 3 times.

17th row: K2, Inc 1, yf, sl 1, k1, psso, yf, Work 5tog, yf, k2tog, yf, Inc 1, k3, yf, sl 2, k1, p2sso, yf, sl 1, k1, psso, yf, k1.

19th row: K4, Inc 1, yf, Work 5tog, yf, Inc 1, k5, yf, k2tog, yf, sl 2, k1, p2sso, yf, k1.

21st row: K6, Cluster 3, k7, yf, sl 2, k1, p2sso, yf, sl 1, k1, psso, yf, k1.

23rd row: K4, k3tog, yf, Inc 2, yf, k3tog tbl, k5, yf, k2tog, yf, sl 2, k1, p2sso, yf, k1.

25th row: K2, k3tog, yf, k2tog, yf, Inc 2, yf, sl 1, k1, psso, yf, k3tog tbl, k3, yf, sl 2, k1, p2sso, yf, sl 1, k1, psso, yf, k1.

27th row: K1, [k2tog, yf] 3 times, k1, [yf, sl 1, k1, psso] 3 times, k2, yf, k2tog, yf, sl 2, k1, p2sso, yf, k1.

28th row: Purl.

Rep these 28 rows.

Snakes and Ladders

Multiple of 8 + 2.

1st row (right side): K7, *k2tog, yf, k6; rep from * to last 3 sts, k2tog, yf, k1.

2nd row: K2, *yfrn, p2tog, k6; rep from * to end.

3rd row: K5, *k2tog, yf, k6; rep from * to last 5 sts, k2tog, yf, k3.

4th row: K4, *yfrn, p2tog, k6; rep from * to last 6 sts, yfrn, p2tog, k4.

5th row: K3, *k2tog, yf, k6; rep from * to last 7 sts, k2tog, yf, k5.

6th row: *K6, yfrn, p2tog; rep from * to last 2 sts, k2.

7th row: K1, *k2tog, yf, k6; rep from * to last st, k1.

8th row: K7, *p2tog tbl, yon, k6; rep from * to last 3 sts, p2tog tbl, yon, k1.

9th row: K2, *yf, k2tog tbl, k6; rep from * to end.

10th row: K5, *p2tog tbl, yon, k6; rep from * to last 5 sts, p2tog tbl, yon, k3.

11th row: K4, *yf, k2tog tbl, k6; rep from * to last 6 sts, yf, k2tog tbl, k4.

12th row: K3, *p2tog tbl, yon, k6; rep from * to last 7 sts, p2tog tbl, yon, k5.

13th row: *K6, yf, k2tog tbl; rep from * to last 2 sts, k2.

14th row: K1, *p2tog tbl, yon, k6; rep from * to last st, k1.

Rep these 14 rows.

Trellis Pattern

Multiple of 4 + 2.

1st row (right side): K1, yf, *sl 1, k1, psso, k2tog, [yfon] twice (2 sts made); rep from * to last 5 sts, sl 1, k1, psso, k2tog, yf, k1.

2nd row: K2, p2, *k into front of first loop of double yfon, then k into back of 2nd loop, p2; rep from * to last 2 sts, k2.

3rd row: K1, p1, *C2B, p2; rep from * to last 4 sts, C2B, p1, k1.

4th row: K2, *p2, k2; rep from * to end.

5th row: K1, k2tog, *[yfon] twice, sl 1, k1, psso, k2tog; rep from * to last 3 sts, [yfon] twice, sl 1, k1, psso, k1.

6th row: K1, p1, k into front of first loop of double yfon, then k into back of 2nd loop, *p2, work into double yfon as before; rep from * to last 2 sts, p1, k1.

7th row: K2, *p2, C2B; rep from * to last 4 sts, p2, k2.

8th row: K1, p1, k2, *p2, k2; rep from * to last 2 sts, p1, k1.
Rep these 8 rows.

Rhombus Lace

Multiple of 8 + 2.

1st row (right side): K1, [k2tog, yf] twice, *k4, [k2tog, yf] twice; rep from * to last 5 sts, k5.

2nd and every alt row: Purl.

3rd row: [K2tog, yf] twice, *k4, [k2tog, yf] twice; rep from * to last 6 sts, k6.

5th row: K1, k2tog, yf, k4, *[k2tog, yf] twice, k4; rep from * to last 3 sts, k2tog, yf, k1.

7th row: K3, [k2tog, yf] twice, *k4, [k2tog, yf] twice; rep from * to last 3 sts, k3.

9th row: K2, *[k2tog, yf] twice, k4; rep from * to end.

11th row: As 1st row.

13th row: K5, [k2tog, yf] twice, *k4, [k2tog, yf] twice; rep from * to last st, k1.

15th row: *K4, [k2tog, yf] twice; rep from * to last 2 sts, k2.

17th row: As 7th row.

19th row: As 5th row.

21st row: K2tog, yf, k4, *[k2tog, yf] twice, k4; rep from * to last 4 sts, k2tog, yf, k2.

23rd row: As 13th row.

24th row: Purl.

Rep these 24 rows.

Fountains Panel

Worked over 16 sts on a background of St st.

1st row (right side): K1, yf, k1, sl 1, k1, psso, p1, k2tog, k1, yfrn, p1, yb, sl 1, k1, psso, p1, k2tog, [yf, k1] twice.

2nd row: P5, k1, p1, k1, p3, k1, p4.

3rd row: K1, yf, k1, sl 1, k1, psso, p1, k2tog, k1, p1, yb, sl 1, k2tog, psso, yf, k3, yf, k1.

4th row: P7, k1, p2, k1, p4.

5th row: [K1, yf] twice, sl 1, k1, psso, p1, [k2tog] twice, yf, k5, yf, k1.

6th row: P8, k1, p1, k1, p5.

7th row: K1, yf, k3, yf, sl 1, k2tog, psso, p1, yon, k1, sl 1, k1, psso, p1, k2tog, k1, yf, k1.

8th row: P4, k1, p3, k1, p7.

9th row: K1, yf, k5, yf, sl 1, k1, psso, k1, sl 1, k1, psso, p1, k2tog, k1, yf, k1.

10th row: P4, k1, p2, k1, p8.

Rep these 10 rows.

Travelling Vine

Multiple of 8 + 2.

Note: Sts should only be counted after WS rows.

1st row (right side): K1, *yf, KB1, yf, k2tog tbl, k5; rep from * to last st, k1.

2nd row: P5, *p2tog tbl, p7; rep from * to last 6 sts, p2tog tbl, p4.

3rd row: K1, *yf, KB1, yf, k2, k2tog tbl, k3; rep from * to last st, k1.

4th row: P3, *p2tog tbl, p7; rep from * to last 8 sts, p2tog tbl, p6.

5th row: K1, *KB1, yf, k4, k2tog tbl, k1, yf; rep from * to last st, k1.

6th row: P2, *p2tog tbl, p7; rep from * to end.

7th row: K6, *k2tog, yf, KB1, yf, k5; rep from * to last 4 sts, k2tog, yf, KB1, yf, k1.

8th row: P4, *p2tog, p7; rep from * to last 7 sts, p2tog, p5.

9th row: K4, *k2tog, k2, yf, KB1, yf, k3; rep from * to last 6 sts, k2tog, k2, yf, KB1, yf, k1.

10th row: P6, *p2tog, p7; rep from * to last 5 sts, p2tog, p3.

11th row: K1, *yf, k1, k2tog, k4, yf, KB1; rep from * to last st, k1.

12th row: *P7, p2tog; rep from * to last 2 sts, p2.

Rep these 12 rows.

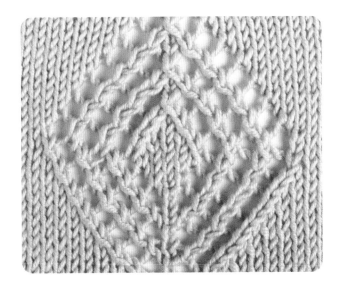

Diamond Medallion Panel

Worked over 17 sts on a background of St st.

1st row (right side): K6, k2tog, yf, k1, yf, sl 1, k1, psso, k6.

2nd and every alt row: Purl.

3rd row: K5, k2tog, yf, k3, yf, sl 1, k1, psso, k5.

5th row: K4, [k2tog, yf] twice, k1, [yf, sl 1, k1, psso] twice, k4.

7th row: K3, [k2tog, yf] twice, k3, [yf, sl 1, k1, psso] twice, k3.

9th row: K2, [k2tog, yf] 3 times, k1, [yf, sl 1, k1, psso] 3 times, k2.

11th row: K1, [k2tog, yf] 3 times, k3, [yf, sl 1, k1, psso] 3 times, k1.

13th row: [K2tog, yf] 3 times, k5, [yf, sl 1, k1, psso] 3 times.

15th row: K1, [yf, sl 1, k1, psso] 3 times, k3, [k2tog, yf] 3 times, k1.

17th row: K2, [yf, sl 1, k1, psso] 3 times, k1, [k2tog, yf] 3 times, k2.

19th row: K3, [yf, sl 1, k1, psso] twice, yf, sl 1, k2tog, psso, yf, [k2tog, yf] twice, k3.

21st row: K4, [yf, sl 1, k1, psso] twice, k1, [k2tog, yf] twice, k4.

23rd row: K5, yf, sl 1, k1, psso, yf, sl 1, k2tog, psso, yf, k2tog, yf, k5.

25th row: K6, yf, sl 1, k1, psso, k1, k2tog, yf, k6.

27th row: K7, yf, sl 1, k2tog, psso, yf, k7.

28th row: Purl.

Rep these 28 rows.

3rd row: K2, p7, *k1, k2tog, yf, k1, yf, sl 1, k1, psso, k1, p7; rep from * to last 2 sts, k2.

5th row: K2, p7, *k2tog, yf, k3, yf, sl 1, k1, psso, p7; rep from * to last 2 sts, k2.

7th row: K2, p7, *k2, yf, sl 1, k2tog, psso, yf, k2, p7; rep from * to last 2 sts, k2.

9th row: As 1st row.

11th row: P2, k3, yf, sl 1, k1, psso, k2, *p7, k3, yf, sl 1, k1, psso, k2; rep from * to last 2 sts, p2.

12th, 14th, 16th, and 18th rows: K2, p7, *k7, p7; rep from * to last 2 sts, k2.

13th row: P2, k1, k2tog, yf, k1, yf, sl 1, k1, psso, k1, *p7, k1, k2tog, yf, k1, yf, sl 1, k1, psso, k1; rep from * to last 2 sts, p2.

15th row: P2, k2tog, yf, k3, yf, sl 1, k1, psso, *p7, k2tog, yf, k3, yf, sl 1, k1, psso; rep from * to last 2 sts, p2.

17th row: P2, k2, yf, sl 1, k2tog, psso, yf, k2, *p7, k2, yf, sl 1, k2tog, psso, yf, k2; rep from * to last 2 sts, p2.

19th row: As 11th row.

20th row: K2, p7, *k7, p7; rep from * to last 2 sts, k2.
Rep these 20 rows.

Eyelet Boxes

Multiple of 14 + 11.

1st row (right side): K2, p7, *k3, yf, sl 1, k1, psso, k2, p7; rep from * to last 2 sts, k2.

2nd, 4th, 6th, 8th, and 10th rows: P2, k7, *p7, k7; rep from * to last 2 sts, p2.

Diagonal Ridges

Multiple of 5 + 2.

1st row (right side): K2tog, yf, *k3, k2tog, yf; rep from * to last 5 sts, k5.

2nd row: P2, *k3, p2; rep from * to end.

3rd row: K4, k2tog, yf, *k3, k2tog, yf; rep from * to last st, k1.

4th row: K1, *p2, k3; rep from * to last st, p1.

5th row: *K3, k2tog, yf; rep from * to last 2 sts, k2.

6th row: K2, *p2, k3; rep from * to end.

7th row: K2, *k2tog, yf, k3; rep from * to end.

8th row: *K3, p2; rep from * to last 2 sts, k2.

9th row: K1, k2tog, yf, *k3, k2tog, yf; rep from * to last 4 sts, k4.

10th row: P1, *k3, p2; rep from * to last st, k1.

Rep these 10 rows.

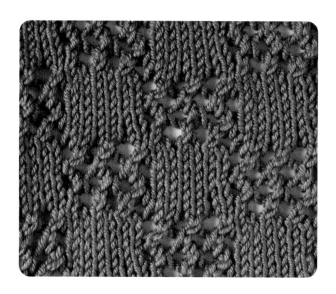

Checkerboard Lace

Multiple of 12 + 8.

1st row (right side): K7, *[yf, k2tog] 3 times, k6; rep from * to last st, k1.

2nd and every alt row: Purl.

3rd row: K7, *[k2tog, yf] 3 times, k6; rep from * to last st, k1.

5th row: As 1st row.

7th row: As 3rd row.

9th row: K1, *[yf, k2tog] 3 times, k6; rep from * to last 7 sts, [yf, k2tog] 3 times, k1.

11th row: K1, *[k2tog, yf] 3 times, k6; rep from * to last 7 sts, [k2tog, yf] 3 times, k1.

13th row: As 9th row.

15th row: As 11th row.

16th row: Purl.

Rep these 16 rows.

Shetland Eyelet Panel

Worked over 9 sts on a background of St st.

1st row (right side): K2, k2tog, yf, k1, yf, sl 1, k1, psso, k2.

2nd and every alt row: Purl.

3rd row: K1, k2tog, yf, k3, yf, sl 1, k1, psso, k1.

5th row: K1, yf, sl 1, k1, psso, yf, sl 2 knitwise, k1, p2sso, yf, k2tog, yf, k1.

7th row: K3, yf, sl 2 knitwise, k1, p2sso, yf, k3.

8th row: Purl.

Rep these 8 rows.

Climbing Leaf Pattern

Multiple of 16 + 1.

1st row (right side): K1, *yf, k5, k2tog, k1, k2tog tbl, k5, yf, k1; rep from * to end.

2nd and every alt row: Purl.

3rd row: As 1st row.

5th row: K1, *k2tog tbl, k5, yf, k1, yf, k5, k2tog, k1; rep from * to end.

7th row: As 5th row.

8th row: Purl.

Rep these 8 rows.

Twin Leaf Lace Panel

Worked over 23 sts on a background of St st.

1st row (right side): K8, k2tog, yf, k1, p1, k1, yf, sl 1, k1, psso, k8.

2nd row: P7, p2tog tbl, p2, yon, k1, yfrn, p2, p2tog, p7.

3rd row: K6, k2tog, k1, yf, k2, p1, k2, yf, k1, sl 1, k1, psso, k6.

4th row: P5, p2tog tbl, p3, yrn, p1, k1, p1, yrn, p3, p2tog, p5.

5th row: K4, k2tog, k2, yf, k3, p1, k3, yf, k2, sl 1, k1, psso, k4.

6th row: P3, p2tog tbl, p4, yrn, p2, k1, p2, yrn, p4, p2tog, p3.

7th row: K2, k2tog, k3, yf, k4, p1, k4, yf, k3, sl 1, k1, psso, k2.

8th row: P1, p2tog tbl, p5, yrn, p3, k1, p3, yrn, p5, p2tog, p1.

9th row: K2tog, k4, yf, k5, p1, k5, yf, k4, sl 1, k1, psso.

10th row: P11, k1, p11.

11th row: K11, p1, k11.

12th row: P11, k1, p11.

Rep these 12 rows.

Lacy Diagonals

Multiple of 6 + 1.

1st row (right side): *K1, k2tog, yf, k1, yf, k2tog tbl; rep from * to last st, k1.

2nd and every alt row: Purl.

3rd row: K2tog, *yf, k3, yf, [sl 1] twice, k1, p2sso; rep from * to last 5 sts, yf, k3, yf, k2tog tbl.

5th row: *K1, yf, k2tog tbl, k1, k2tog, yf; rep from * to last st, k1.

7th row: K2, *yf, [sl 1] twice, k1, p2sso, yf, k3; rep from * to last 5 sts, yf, [sl 1] twice, k1, p2sso, yf, k2.

8th row: Purl.

Rep these 8 rows.

If you are a tight knitter, make sure that you form the new stitches around the fullest part of your needles when lace knitting.

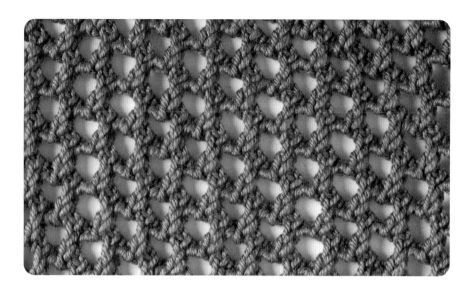

Fancy Openwork

Multiple of 4.

Note: Sts should only be counted after the 2nd and 4th rows.

1st row (right side): K2, *yf, k4; rep from * to last 2 sts, yf, k2.

2nd row: P2tog, *(k1, p1) into the yf of the previous row, [p2tog] twice; rep from * to last 3 sts, (k1, p1) into the yf, p2tog.

3rd row: K4, *yf, k4; rep from * to end.

4th row: P2, p2tog, *(k1, p1) into the yf of previous row, [p2tog] twice; rep from * to last 5 sts, (k1, p1) into the yf, p2tog, p2.

Rep these 4 rows.

Vertical Ripple Stripes

Multiple of 5 + 3.

Note: Do not count yf and sts resulting from yf as a stitch.

1st Foundation row (right side): K3, *yf, k4; rep from * to end.

2nd, 3rd and 4th Foundation rows: Work 3 rows in st st, starting purl.

1st row: *K5, yf; rep from * to last 3 sts, k3.

2nd and every alt row: Purl.

3rd row: K3, *slip next st off left-hand needle and allow it to drop down to the loop made 6 rows below, k5, rep from * to end.

5th row: K3, *yf, k5; rep from * to end.

7th row: *K5, slip next st off left-hand needle as before; rep from * to last 3 sts, k3.

8th row: Purl.

Rep the last 8 rows.

Florette Pattern

Multiple of 12 + 7.

1st row (right side): K1, *p2tog, yon, k1, yfrn, p2tog, k7; rep from * to last 6 sts, p2tog, yon, k1, yfrn, p2tog, k1.

2nd and every alt row: Purl.

3rd row: K1, *yfrn, p2tog, k1, p2tog, yon, k7; rep from * to last 6 sts, yfrn, p2tog, k1, p2tog, yon, k1.

5th row: As 3rd row.

7th row: As 1st row.

9th row: K7, *p2tog, yon, k1, yfrn, p2tog, k7; rep from * to end.

11th row: K7, *yfrn, p2tog, k1, p2tog, yon, k7; rep from * to end.

13th row: As 11th row.

15th row: As 9th row.

16th row: Purl.

Rep these 16 rows.

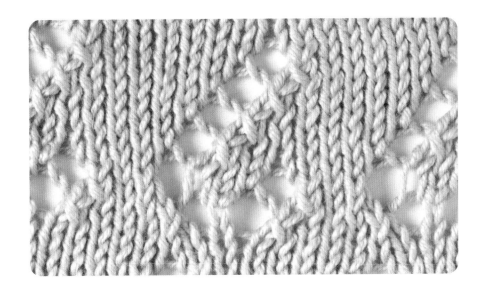

Fish Hooks

Multiple of 8 + 1.

1st row and every alt row (wrong side): Purl.

2nd row: Knit.

4th row: K2, sl 1, k1, psso, yf, k1, yf, k2tog, *k3, sl 1, k1, psso, yf, k1, yf, k2tog; rep from * to last 2 sts, k2.

6th row: K1, *sl 1, k1, psso, yf, k3, yf, k2tog, k1; rep from * to end.

8th row: K4, sl 1, k1, psso, yf, *k6, sl 1, k1, psso, yf; rep from * to last 3 sts, k3.

10th row: K3, sl 1, k1, psso, yf, *k6, sl 1, k1, psso, yf; rep from * to last 4 sts, k4.

12th row: K2, sl 1, k1, psso, yf, *k6, sl 1, k1, psso, yf; rep from * to last 5 sts, k5.

14th row: K1, *sl 1, k1, psso, yf, k6; rep from * to end.

16th row: Knit.

18th row: As 4th row.

20th row: As 6th row.

22nd row: K3, yf, k2tog, *k6, yf, k2tog; rep from * to last 4 sts, k4.

24th row: K4, yf, k2tog, *k6, yf, k2tog; rep from * to last 3 sts, k3.

26th row: K5, yf, k2tog, *k6, yf, k2tog; rep from * to last 2 sts, k2.

28th row: *K6, yf, k2tog; rep from * to last st, k1.

Rep these 28 rows.

Shetland Fern Panel

Worked over 13 sts on a background of St st.

1st row (right side): K6, yf, sl 1, k1, psso, k5.

2nd row: Purl.

3rd row: K4, k2tog, yf, k1, yf, sl 1, k1, psso, k4.

4th row: Purl.

5th row: K3, k2tog, yf, k3, yf, sl 1, k1, psso, k3.

6th row: Purl.

7th row: K3, yf, sl 1, k1, psso, yf, sl 1, k2tog, psso, yf, k2tog, yf, k3.

8th row: Purl.

9th row: K1, k2tog, yf, k1, yf, sl 1, k1, psso, k1, k2tog, yf, k1, yf, sl 1, k1, psso, k1.

10th row: Purl.

11th row: K1, [yf, sl 1, k1, psso] twice, k3, [k2tog, yf] twice, k1.

12th row: P2, [yrn, p2tog] twice, p1, [p2tog tbl, yrn] twice, p2.

13th row: K3, yf, sl 1, k1, psso, yf, sl 1, k2tog, psso, yf, k2tog, yf, k3.

14th row: P4, yrn, p2tog, p1, p2tog tbl, yrn, p4.

15th row: K5, yf, sl 1, k2tog, psso, yf, k5.

16th row: Purl.

Rep these 16 rows.

Diamond Diagonal

Multiple of 8 + 2.

1st row (right side): K1, *yf, k2tog tbl, k6; rep from * to last st, k1.

2nd row: K1, *yfrn, p2tog, k3, p2tog tbl, yon, k1; rep from * to last st, k1.

3rd row: *K3, yf, k2tog tbl, k1, k2tog, yf; rep from * to last 2 sts, k2.

4th row: K3, *yfrn, p3tog tbl, yon, k5; rep from * to last 7 sts, yfrn, p3tog tbl, yon, k4.

5th row: K5, *yf, k2tog tbl, k6; rep from * to last 5 sts, yf, k2tog tbl, k3.

6th row: K2, *p2tog tbl, yon, k1, yfrn, p2tog, k3; rep from * to end.

7th row: K2, *k2tog, yf, k3, yf, k2tog tbl, k1; rep from * to end.

8th row: P2tog tbl, *yon, k5, yfrn, p3tog tbl; rep from * to last 8 sts, yon, k5, yfrn, p2tog, k1.

Rep these 8 rows.

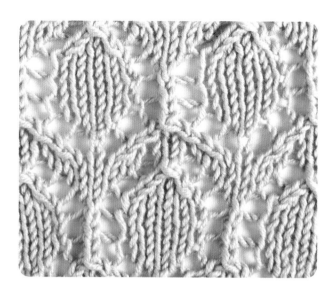

Cogwheel Eyelets

Multiple of 8 + 1.

1st row (right side): K2, k2tog, yf, k1, yf, sl 1, k1, psso, *k3, k2tog, yf, k1, yf, sl 1, k1, psso; rep from * to last 2 sts, k2.

2nd and every alt row: Purl.

3rd row: K1, *k2tog, yf, k3, yf, sl 1, k1, psso, k1; rep from * to end.

5th row: K2tog, yf, k5, *yf, sl 1, k2tog, psso, yf, k5; rep from * to last 2 sts, yf, sl 1, k1, psso.

7th row: Sl 1, k1, psso, yf, k5, *yf, sl 2tog knitwise, k1, p2sso, yf, k5; rep from * to last 2 sts, yf, k2tog.

9th row: As 7th row.

11th row: K2, yf, sl 1, k1, psso, k1, k2tog, yf, *k3, yf, sl 1, k1, psso, k1, k2tog, yf; rep from * to last 2 sts, k2.

13th row: K3, yf, sl 1, k2tog, psso, yf, *k5, yf, sl 1, k2tog, psso, yf; rep from * to last 3 sts, k3.

15th row: K1, *yf, sl 1, k1, psso, k3, k2tog, yf, k1; rep from * to end.

17th row: As 11th row.

19th row: As 13th row.

21st row: K3, yf, sl 2tog knitwise, k1, p2sso, yf, *k5, yf, sl 2tog knitwise, k1, p2sso, yf; rep from * to last 3 sts, k3.

23rd row: As 21st row.

25th row: As 3rd row.

27th row: As 5th row.

28th row: Purl.

Rep these 28 rows.

Bell Lace

Multiple of 8 + 3.

1st row (right side): K1, p1, k1, *p1, yon, sl 1, k2tog, psso, yfrn, [p1, k1] twice; rep from * to end.

2nd row: P1, k1, p1, *k1, p3, [k1, p1] twice; rep from * to end.

Rep last 2 rows twice more.

7th row: K1, k2tog, *yfrn, [p1, k1] twice, p1, yon, sl 1, k2tog, psso; rep from * to last 8 sts, yfrn, [p1, k1] twice, p1, yon, sl 1, k1, psso, k1.

8th row: P3, *[k1, p1] twice, k1, p3; rep from * to end.

Rep the last 2 rows twice more.

Rep these 12 rows.

Experiment with hand-painted yarns for lace knitting – the key is to keep the pattern simple.

2nd row: P4, k2, p2, k2, *p3, k2, p2, k2; rep from * to last 4 sts, p4.

3rd row: K4, p2, k2, p2, *k3, p2, k2, p2; rep from * to last 4 sts, k4.

Rep the last 2 rows twice more.

8th row: P2, drop next st down 7 rows, *p1, k2, p2, k2, p1, drop next st down 7 rows; rep from * to last 2 sts, p2.

9th row: K3, p2, *k2, p2; rep from * to last 3 sts, k3.

10th row: P3, k2, *p2, k2; rep from * to last 3 sts, p3.

11th row: K3, p2, k1, M1, k1, p2, *k2, p2, k1, M1, k1, p2; rep from * to last 3 sts, k3.

12th row: P3, k2, p3, k2, *p2, k2, p3, k2; rep from * to last 3 sts, p3.

13th row: K3, p2, k3, p2, *k2, p2, k3, p2; rep from * to last 3 sts, k3.

Rep the last 2 rows twice more.

18th row: P3, k2, p1, drop next st down 7 rows, p1, k2, *p2, k2, p1, drop next st down 7 rows, p1, k2; rep from * to last 3 sts, p3.

19th row: K3, p2, *k2, p2; rep from * to last 3 sts, k3.

20th row: P3, k2, *p2, k2; rep from * to last 3 sts, p3.

Rep these 20 rows.

Snow Shoe Pattern

Multiple of 8 + 4.

Note: Sts should only be counted after the 8th, 9th, 10th, 18th, 19th or 20th rows.

1st row (right side): K2, M1, *k1, p2, k2, p2, k1, M1; rep from * to last 2 sts, k2.

Gothic Windows

Multiple of 8 + 2.

Note: Sts should not be counted after the 3rd, 7th, 9th and 11th rows.

1st row (right side): P4, *k2, p6; rep from * to last 6 sts, k2, p4.

2nd row: K4, *p2, k6; rep from * to last 6 sts, p2, k4.

3rd row: P3, *k2tog, yf, sl 1, k1, psso, p4; rep from * to last 7 sts, k2tog, yf, sl 1, k1, psso, p3.

4th row: K3, *p1, k into back then front of next st, p1, k4; rep from * to last 6 sts, p1, k into back then front of next st, p1, k3.

5th row: P2, *k2tog, yf, k2, yf, sl 1, k1, psso, p2; rep from * to end.

6th row: K2, *p6, k2; rep from * to end.

7th row: K1, *k2tog, yf, k2tog, [yf, sl 1, k1, psso] twice; rep from * to last st, k1.

8th row: P4, *k into front then back of next st, p6; rep from * to last 5 sts, k into front then back of next st, p4.

9th row: K1, *[yf, sl 1, k1, psso] twice, k2tog, yf, k2tog; rep from * to last st, yf, k1.

10th row: K1, KB1, *p6, k into back then front of next st; rep from * to last 8 sts, p6, KB1, k1.

11th row: P2, *yon, k3tog tbl, yf, k3tog, yfrn, p2; rep from * to end.

12th row: K2, *KB1, p1, k into back then front of next st, p1, KB1, k2; rep from * to end.

13th row: P3, *yon, sl 1, k1, psso, k2tog, yfrn, p4; rep from * to last 7 sts, yon, sl 1, k1, psso, k2tog, yfrn, p3.

14th row: K3, *KB1, p2, KB1, k4; rep from * to last 7 sts, KB1, p2, KB1, k3.

Rep these 14 rows.

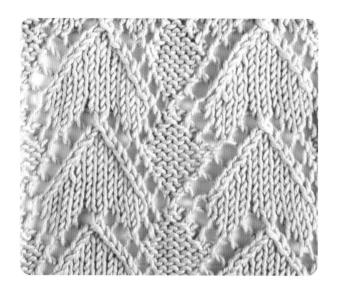

Inverted Hearts

Multiple of 14 + 1.

1st row (right side): P2tog, yon, k11, *yfrn, p3tog, yon, k11; rep from * to last 2 sts, yfrn, p2tog.

2nd row: K1, *p13, k1; rep from * to end.

3rd row: P2, yon, sl 1, k1, psso, k7, *k2tog, yfrn, p3, yon, sl 1, k1, psso, k7; rep from * to last 4 sts, k2tog, yfrn, p2.

4th row: K2, p11, *k3, p11; rep from * to last 2 sts, k2.

5th row: P3, yon, sl 1, k1, psso, k5, k2tog, yfrn, *p5, yon, sl 1, k1, psso, k5, k2tog, yfrn; rep from * to last 3 sts, p3.

6th row: K3, p9, *k5, p9; rep from * to last 3 sts, k3.

7th row: P4, yon, sl 1, k1, psso, k3, k2tog, yfrn, *p7, yon, sl 1, k1, psso, k3, k2tog, yfrn; rep from * to last 4 sts, p4.

8th row: K4, p7, *k7, p7; rep from * to last 4 sts, k4.

9th row: P2, p2tog, yon, k1, yf, sl 1, k1, psso, k1, k2tog, yf, k1, yfrn, p2tog, *p3, p2tog, yon, k1, yf, sl 1, k1, psso, k1, k2tog, yf, k1, yfrn, p2tog; rep from * to last 2 sts, p2.

10th row: As 6th row.

11th row: P1, *p2tog, yon, k3, yf, sl 1, k2tog, psso, yf, k3, yfrn, p2tog, p1; rep from * to end.

12th row: As 4th row.

Rep these 12 rows.

Diamond Trellis

Multiple of 16 + 1.

1st row (right side): K2tog, yf, k12, *[k2tog, yf] twice, k12; rep from * to last 3 sts, k2tog, yf, k1.

2nd and every alt row: Purl.

3rd row: K2, yf, sl 1, k1, psso, k9, *[k2tog, yf] twice, k1, yf, sl 1, k1, psso, k9; rep from * to last 4 sts, k2tog, yf, k2.

5th row: K1, *[yf, sl 1, k1, psso] twice, k7, [k2tog, yf] twice, k1; rep from * to end.

7th row: K2, [yf, sl 1, k1, psso] twice, k5, [k2tog, yf] twice, *k3, [yf, sl 1, k1, psso] twice, k5, [k2tog, yf] twice; rep from * to last 2 sts, k2.

9th row: K3, [yf, sl 1, k1, psso] twice, k3, [k2tog, yf] twice, *k5, [yf, sl 1, k1, psso] twice, k3, [k2tog, yf] twice; rep from * to last 3 sts, k3.

11th row: K4, [yf, sl 1, k1, psso] twice, k1, [k2tog, yf] twice, *k7, [yf, sl 1, k1, psso] twice, k1, [k2tog, yf] twice; rep from * to last 4 sts, k4.

13th row: K5, yf, sl 1, k1, psso, yf, k3tog, yf, k2tog, yf, *k9, yf, sl 1, k1, psso, yf, k3tog, yf, k2tog, yf; rep from * to last 5 sts, k5.

15th row: K6, yf, k3tog, yf, k2tog, yf, *k11, yf, k3tog, yf, k2tog, yf; rep from * to last 6 sts, k6.

17th row: K6, [k2tog, yf] twice, *k12, [k2tog, yf] twice; rep from * to last 7 sts, k7.

19th row: K5, [k2tog, yf] twice, k1, yf, sl 1, k1, psso, *k9, [k2tog, yf] twice, k1, yf, sl 1, k1, psso; rep from * to last 5 sts, k5.

21st row: K4, [k2tog, yf] twice, k1, [yf, sl 1, k1, psso] twice, *k7, [k2tog, yf] twice, k1, [yf, sl 1, k1, psso] twice; rep from * to last 4 sts, k4.

23rd row: K3, [k2tog, yf] twice, k3, [yf, sl 1, k1, psso] twice, *k5, [k2tog, yf] twice, k3, [yf, sl 1, k1, psso] twice; rep from * to last 3 sts, k3.

25th row: K2, [k2tog, yf] twice, k5, [yf, sl 1, k1, psso] twice, *k3, [k2tog, yf] twice, k5, [yf, sl 1, k1, psso] twice; rep from * to last 2 sts, k2.

27th row: *K1, [k2tog, yf] twice, k7, [yf, sl 1, k1, psso] twice; rep from * to last st, k1.

29th row: [K2tog, yf] twice, k9, *yf, sl 1, k1, psso, yf, k3tog, yf, k2tog, yf, k9; rep from * to last 4 sts, [yf, sl 1, k1, psso] twice.

31st row: K1, k2tog, yf, k11, *yf, k3tog, yf, k2tog, yf, k11; rep from * to last 3 sts, yf, k2tog, k1.

32nd row: Purl.

Rep these 32 rows.

Diamond Rib

Multiple of 9 + 2.

1st row (right side): P2, *k2tog, [k1, yf] twice, k1, sl 1, k1, psso, p2; rep from * to end.

2nd and every alt row: K2, *p7, k2; rep from * to end.

3rd row: P2, *k2tog, yf, k3, yf, sl 1, k1, psso, p2; rep from * to end.

5th row: P2, *k1, yf, sl 1, k1, psso, k1, k2tog, yf, k1, p2; rep from * to end.

7th row: P2, *k2, yf, sl 1, k2tog, psso, yf, k2, p2; rep from * to end.

8th row: As 2nd row.

Rep these 8 rows.

Avoid lace knitting with acrylic yarn, which tends to block poorly.

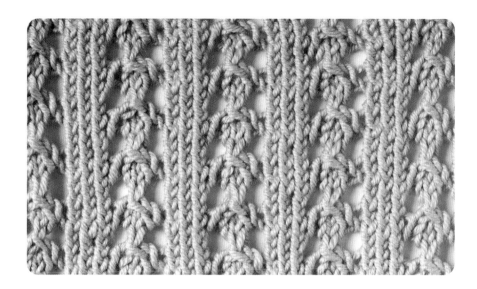

Simple Lace Rib

Multiple of 6 + 1.

1st row (right side): [KB1] twice, *k3, [KB1] 3 times; rep from * to last 5 sts, k3, [KB1] twice.

2nd row: [PB1] twice, *p3, [PB1] 3 times; rep from * to last 5 sts, p3, [PB1] twice.

3rd row: [KB1] twice, *yf, sl 1, k2tog, psso, yf, [KB1] 3 times; rep from * to last 5 sts, yf, sl 1, k2tog, psso, yf, [KB1] twice.

4th row: As 2nd row.

Rep these 4 rows.

Wheatear Stitch

Multiple of 8 + 6.

1st row (right side): P5, *k2, yf, sl 1, k1, psso, p4; rep from * to last st, p1.

2nd row: K5, *p2, yrn, p2tog, k4; rep from * to last st, k1.

Rep the last 2 rows 3 times more.

9th row: P1, *k2, yf, sl 1, k1, psso, p4; rep from * to last 5 sts, k2, yf, sl 1, k1, psso, p1.

10th row: K1, *p2, yrn, p2tog, k4; rep from * to last 5 sts, p2, yrn, p2tog, k1.

Rep the last 2 rows 3 times more.

Rep these 16 rows.

Chalice Cup Panel

Worked over 13 sts on a background of St st.

Note: Sts should not be counted after the 7th, 8th, 15th or 16th rows of this pattern.

1st row (right side): P1, k3, k2tog, yf, k1, yf, sl 1, k1, psso, k3, p1.

2nd row: K1, p11, k1.

3rd row: P1, k2, k2tog, yf, k3, yf, sl 1, k1, psso, k2, p1.

4th row: As 2nd row.

5th row: P1, k1, k2tog, yf, k1, yf, sl 1, k2tog, psso, yf, k1, yf, sl 1, k1, psso, k1, p1.

6th row: As 2nd row.

7th row: P1, k2tog, yf, k3, yf, k1, yf, k3, yf, sl 1, k1, psso, p1.

8th row: K1, p13, k1.

9th row: P1, k2tog, yf, sl 1, k1, psso, k5, k2tog, yf, sl 1, k1, psso, p1.

10th row: As 2nd row.

11th row: P1, k2tog, yf, k1, yf, sl 1, k1, psso, k1, k2tog, yf, k1, yf, sl 1, k1, psso, p1.

12th row: As 2nd row.

Rep the last 2 rows once more.

15th row: P1, k1, yf, k3, yf, sl 1, k2tog, psso, yf, k3, yf, k1, p1.

16th row: As 8th row.

17th row: P1, k3, k2tog, yf, sl 1, k2tog, psso, yf, sl 1, k1, psso, k3, p1.

18th row: As 2nd row.

Rep these 18 rows.

Embossed Rosebud Panel

Worked over 9 sts on a background of reverse St st.

1st row (wrong side): K3, p3, k3.

2nd row: P3, slip next st onto cable needle and hold at front of work, k1, [k1, yf, k1, yf, k1] into next st on left-hand needle, then knit st from cable needle, p3.

3rd row: K3, p1, [KB1] 5 times, p1, k3.

4th row: P3, [k1, yf] 6 times, k1, p3.

5th row: K3, p13, k3.

6th row: P3, k13, p3.

7th row: K3, p2tog, p9, p2tog tbl, k3.

8th row: P3, yb, sl 1, k1, psso, k7, k2tog, p3.

9th row: K3, p2tog, p5, p2tog tbl, k3.

10th row: P3, yb, sl 1, k1, psso, k3, k2tog, p3.

11th row: K3, p2tog, p1, p2tog tbl, k3.

12th row: P3, k3, p3.

Rep these 12 rows.

Staggered Fern Lace Panel

Worked over 20 sts on a background of St st.

1st row (right side): P2, k9, yf, k1, yf, k3, sl 1, k2tog, psso, p2.

2nd and every alt row: Purl.

3rd row: P2, k10, yf, k1, yf, k2, sl 1, k2tog, psso, p2.

5th row: P2, k3tog, k4, yf, k1, yf, k3, [yf, k1] twice, sl 1, k2tog, psso, p2.

7th row: P2, k3tog, k3, yf, k1, yf, k9, p2.

9th row: P2, k3tog, k2, yf, k1, yf, k10, p2.

11th row: P2, k3tog, [k1, yf] twice, k3, yf, k1, yf, k4, sl 1, k2tog, psso, p2.

12th row: Purl.

Rep these 12 rows.

Reversed Diamonds

Multiple of 12 + 1.

1st row (right side): K1, *yf, k3, sl 1, k1, psso, k1, k2tog, k3, yf, k1; rep from * to end.

2nd row: P2, k9, *p3, k9; rep from * to last 2 sts, p2.

3rd row: K2, yf, k2, sl 1, k1, psso, k1, k2tog, k2, yf, *k3, yf, k2, sl 1, k1, psso, k1, k2tog, k2, yf; rep from * to last 2 sts, k2.

4th row: P3, k7, *p5, k7; rep from * to last 3 sts, p3.

5th row: K3, yf, k1, sl 1, k1, psso, k1, k2tog, k1, yf, *k5, yf, k1, sl 1, k1, psso, k1, k2tog, k1, yf; rep from * to last 3 sts, k3.

6th row: P4, k5, *p7, k5; rep from * to last 4 sts, p4.

7th row: K4, yf, sl 1, k1, psso, k1, k2tog, yf, *k7, yf, sl 1, k1, psso, k1, k2tog, yf; rep from * to last 4 sts, k4.

8th row: P5, k3, *p9, k3; rep from * to last 5 sts, p5.

9th row: K5, yf, sl 1, k2tog, psso, yf, *k9, yf, sl 1, k2tog, psso, yf; rep from * to last 5 sts, k5.

10th row: P6, k1, *p11, k1; rep from * to last 6 sts, p6.

11th row: K1, *k2tog, k3, yf, k1, yf, k3, sl 1, k1, psso, k1; rep from * to end.

12th row: As 8th row.

13th row: K1, *k2tog, k2, yf, k3, yf, k2, sl 1, k1, psso, k1; rep from * to end.

14th row: As 6th row.

15th row: K1, *k2tog, k1, yf, k5, k1, sl 1, k1, psso, k1; rep from * to end.

16th row: As 4th row.

17th row: K1, *k2tog, yf, k7, yf, sl 1, k1, psso, k1; rep from * to end.

18th row: As 2nd row.

19th row: K2tog, yf, k9, *yf, sl 1, k2tog, psso, yf, k9; rep from * to last 2 sts, yf, sl 1, k1, psso.

20th row: P1, *k11, p1; rep from * to end.

Rep these 20 rows.

Shadow Triangles

Multiple of 10 + 3.

1st row (right side): K2, yf, sl 1, k1, psso, k5, k2tog, yf, *k1, yf, sl 1, k1, psso, k5, k2tog, yf; rep from * to last 2 sts, k2.

2nd row: P4, k5, *p5, k5; rep from * to last 4 sts, p4.

3rd row: K3, *yf, sl 1, k1, psso, k3, k2tog, yf, k3; rep from * to end.

4th row: P5, k3, *p7, k3; rep from * to last 5 sts, p5.

5th row: K4, yf, sl 1, k1, psso, k1, k2tog, yf, *k5, yf, sl 1, k1, psso, k1, k2tog, yf; rep from * to last 4 sts, k4.

6th row: P6, k1, *p9, k1; rep from * to last 6 sts, p6.

7th row: K5, yf, sl 1, k2tog, psso, yf, *k7, yf, sl 1, k2tog, psso, yf; rep from * to last 5 sts, k5.

8th row: Purl.

9th row: K4, k2tog, yf, k1, yf, sl 1, k1, psso, *k5, k2tog, yf, k1, yf, sl 1, k1, psso; rep from * to last 4 sts, k4.

10th row: K4, p5, *k5, p5; rep from * to last 4 sts, k4.

11th row: K3, *k2tog, yf, k3, yf, sl 1, k1, psso, k3; rep from * to end.

12th row: K3, *p7, k3; rep from * to end.

13th row: K2, k2tog, yf, k5, yf, sl 1, k1, psso, *k1, k2tog, yf, k5, yf, sl 1, k1, psso; rep from * to last 2 sts, k2.

14th row: P1, k1, *p9, k1; rep from * to last st, p1.

15th row: K1, k2tog, yf, k7, *yf, sl 1, k2tog, psso, yf, k7; rep from * to last 3 sts, yf, sl 1, k1, psso, k1.

16th row: Purl.

Rep these 16 rows.

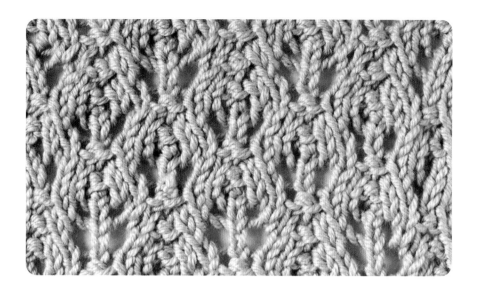

Flower Buds

Multiple of 8 + 5.

1st row (right side): K3, *yf, k2, p3tog, k2, yf, k1; rep from * to last 2 sts, k2.

2nd row: Purl.

Rep the last 2 rows twice more.

7th row: K2, p2tog, *k2, yf, k1, yf, k2, p3tog; rep from * to last 9 sts, k2, yf, k1, yf, k2, p2tog, k2.

8th row: Purl.

Rep the last 2 rows twice more.

Rep these 12 rows.

As a beginner, avoid working with novelty and fuzzy yarns as they can make stitches difficult to see.

Puff Stitch Check 1

Multiple of 10 + 7.

Special Abbreviation: K5W = knit next 5 sts wrapping yarn twice around needle for each st.

1st row (right side): P6, k5W, *p5, k5W; rep from * to last 6 sts, p6.

2nd row: K6, p5 dropping extra loops, *k5, p5 dropping extra loops; rep from * to last 6 sts, k6.

Rep the last 2 rows 3 times more.

9th row: P1, k5W, *p5, k5W; rep from * to last st, p1.

10th row: K1, p5 dropping extra loops, *k5, p5 dropping extra loops; rep from * to last st, k1.

Rep the last 2 rows 3 times more.

Rep these 16 rows.

Cascading Leaves

Worked over 16 sts on a background of reverse St st.

1st row (right side): P1, k3, k2tog, k1, yfrn, p2, yon, k1, sl 1, k1, psso, k3, p1.

2nd and every alt row: K1, p6, k2, p6, k1.

3rd row: P1, k2, k2tog, k1, yf, k1, p2, k1, yf, k1, sl 1, k1, psso, k2, p1.

5th row: P1, k1, k2tog, k1, yf, k2, p2, k2, yf, k1, sl 1, k1, psso, k1, p1.

7th row: P1, k2tog, k1, yf, k3, p2, k3, yf, k1, sl 1, k1, psso, p1.

8th row: K1, p6, k2, p6, k1.

Rep these 8 rows.

Travelling Ribbed
Eyelet Panel

Worked over 13 sts on a background of St st.

1st row (right side): K2, p2, yon, sl 1, k1, psso, k1, k2tog, yfrn, p2, k2.

2nd row: K4, p5, k4.

Rep the last 2 rows twice more.

7th row: K2, p2, k5, p2, k2.

8th row: As 2nd row.

9th row: K2, p2, k2tog, yf, k1, yf, sl 1, k1, psso, p2, k2.

10th row: As 2nd row.

Rep the last two rows twice more.

15th row: As 7th row.

16th row: As 2nd row.

Rep these 16 rows.

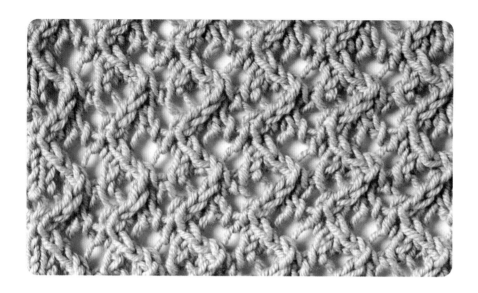

Zigzag Lace

Multiple of 4 + 3.

1st row (right side): K4, *k2tog, yf, k2; rep from * to last 3 sts, k2tog, yf, k1.

2nd row: *P2, yrn, p2tog; rep from * to last 3 sts, p3.

3rd row: *K2, k2tog, yf; rep from * to last 3 sts, k3.

4th row: P4, *yrn, p2tog, p2; rep from * to last 3 sts, yrn, p2tog, p1.

5th row: K1, *yf, sl 1, k1, psso, k2; rep from * to last 2 sts, k2.

6th row: P3, *p2tog tbl, yrn, p2; rep from * to end.

7th row: K3, *yf, sl 1, k1, psso, k2; rep from * to end.

8th row: P1, *p2tog tbl, yrn, p2; rep from * to last 2 sts, p2.

Rep these 8 rows.

Faggotting

Multiple of 3.

Note: Sts should only be counted after the 2nd and 4th rows.

1st row (right side): *K1, [yf] twice, k2tog; rep from * to end.

2nd row: P1, *purl into first yf of previous row, drop second yf off needle, p2; rep from * to last 3 sts, purl into first yf, drop second yf off needle, p1.

3rd row: *K2tog, [yf] twice, k1; rep from * to end.

4th row: As 2nd row.

Rep these 4 rows.

Little and Large Diamonds

Multiple of 12 + 1.

1st row (right side): K1, *yf, sl 1, k1, psso, k7, k2tog, yf, k1; rep from * to end.

2nd and every alt row: Purl.

3rd row: K2, yf, sl 1, k1, psso, k5, *k2tog, yf, k3, yf, sl 1, k1, psso, k5; rep from * to last 4 sts, k2tog, yf, k2.

5th row: K3, yf, sl 1, k1, psso, k3, *k2tog, yf, k5, yf, sl 1, k1, psso, k3; rep from * to last 5 sts, k2tog, yf, k3.

7th row: *K1, k2tog, yf, k1, yf, sl 1, k1, psso; rep from * to last st, k1.

9th row: K2tog, yf, k3, *yf, sl 1, k2tog, psso, yf, k3; rep from * to last 2 sts, yf, sl 1, k1, psso.

11th row: K4, k2tog, yf, k1, yf, sl 1, k1, psso, *k7, k2tog, yf, k1, yf, sl 1, k1, psso; rep from * to last 4 sts, k4.

13th row: K3, k2tog, yf, k3, yf, sl 1, k1, psso, *k5, k2tog, yf, k3, yf, sl 1, k1, psso; rep from * to last 3 sts, k3.

15th row: K2, k2tog, yf, k5, yf, sl 1, k1, psso, *k3, k2tog, yf, k5, yf, sl 1, k1, psso; rep from * to last 2 sts, k2.

17th row: As 7th row.

19th row: As 9th row.

20th row: Purl.

Rep these 20 rows.

Puff Stitch Check II

Work as Puff Stitch Check I on page 167, using reverse side as right side.

When lace knitting, light-weight yarns create a gossamer-like effect. The thicker your yarn is, the thicker the lace will be.

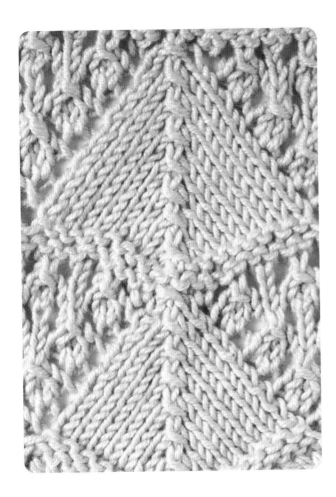

Pyramid Lace Panel

Worked over 25 sts on a background of St st.

1st row (right side): Purl.

2nd row: Knit.

3rd row: K3, yf, k8, sl 1, k2tog, psso, k8, yf, k3.

4th and every following alt row to 18th row: Purl.

5th row: K4, yf, k7, sl 1, k2tog, psso, k7, yf, k4.

7th row: K2, k2tog, yf, k1, yf, k6, sl 1, k2tog, psso, k6, yf, k1, yf, sl 1, k1, psso, k2.

9th row: K6, yf, k5, sl 1, k2tog, psso, k5, yf, k6.

11th row: K3, yf, sl 1, k2tog, psso, yf, k1, yf, k4, sl 1, k2tog, psso, k4, yf, k1, yf, sl 1, k2tog, psso, yf, k3.

13th row: K8, yf, k3, sl 1, k2tog, psso, k3, yf, k8.

15th row: K2, k2tog, yf, k1, yf, sl 1, k2tog, psso, yf, k1, yf, k2, sl 1, k2tog, psso, k2, yf, k1, yf, sl 1, k2tog, psso, yf, k1, yf, sl 1, k1, psso, k2.

17th row: K10, yf, k1, sl 1, k2tog, psso, k1, yf, k10.

19th row: K3, [yf, sl 1, k2tog, psso, yf, k1] 4 times, yf, sl 1, k2tog, psso, yf, k3.

20th row: Knit.

Rep these 20 rows.

Lacy Diamonds

Multiple of 6 + 1.

1st row (right side): *K1, k2tog, yf, k1, yf, k2tog tbl; rep from * to last st, k1.

2nd and every alt row: Purl.

3rd row: K2tog, *yf, k3, yf, [sl 1] twice, k1, p2sso; rep from * to last 5 sts, yf, k3, yf, k2tog tbl.

5th row: *K1, yf, k2tog tbl, k1, k2tog, yf; rep from * to last st, k1.

7th row: K2, *yf, [sl 1] twice, k1, p2sso, yf, k3; rep from * to last 5 sts, yf, [sl 1] twice, k1, p2sso, yf, k2.

8th row: Purl.

Rep these 8 rows.

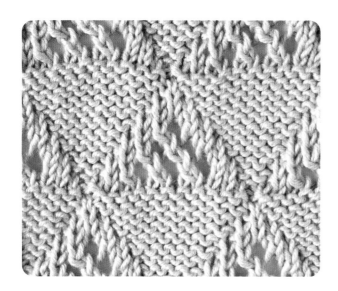

Eyelet Pyramids

Multiple of 12 + 3.

1st row (right side): P2, k11, *p1, k11; rep from * to last 2 sts, p2.

2nd row: K2, p11, *k1, p11; rep from * to last 2 sts, k2.

3rd row: *P3, k2, [yf, sl 1, k1, psso] 3 times, k1; rep from * to last 3 sts, p3.

4th row: K3, *p9, k3; rep from * to end.

5th row: P4, k2, [yf, sl 1, k1, psso] twice, k1, *p5, k2, [yf, sl 1, k1, psso] twice, k1; rep from * to last 4 sts, p4.

6th row: K4, p7, *k5, p7; rep from * to last 4 sts, k4.

7th row: P5, k2, yf, sl 1, k1, psso, k1, *p7, k2, yf, sl 1, k1, psso, k1; rep from * to last 5 sts, p5.

8th row: K5, p5, *k7, p5; rep from * to last 5 sts, k5.

9th row: P6, k3, *p9, k3; rep from * to last 6 sts, p6.

10th row: K6, p3, *k9, p3; rep from * to last 6 sts, k6.

11th row: P7, k1, *p11, k1; rep from * to last 7 sts, p7.

12th row: K7, p1, *k11, p1; rep from * to last 7 sts, k7.

13th row: As 12th row.

14th row: As 11th row.

15th row: K1, [yf, sl 1, k1, psso] twice, k1, p3, *k2, [yf, sl 1, k1, psso] 3 times, k1, p3; rep from * to last 6 sts, k2, yf, sl 1, k1, psso, k2.

16th row: As 9th row.

17th row: K2, yf, sl 1, k1, psso, k1, p5, *k2, [yf, sl 1, k1, psso] twice, k1, p5; rep from * to last 5 sts, k2, yf, sl 1, k1, psso, k1.

18th row: P5, k5, *p7, k5; rep from * to last 5 sts, p5.

19th row: K1, yf, sl 1, k1, psso, k1, p7, *k2, yf, sl 1, k1, psso, k1, p7; rep from * to last 4 sts, k2, yf, sl 1, k1, psso.

20th row: P4, k7, *p5, k7; rep from * to last 4 sts, p4.

21st row: As 4th row.

22nd row: P3, *k9, p3; rep from * to end.

23rd row: As 2nd row.

24th row: As 1st row.

Rep these 24 rows.

Eyelet Ribs

Multiple of 11 + 4.

1st row (right side): K1, yfrn, p2tog, k1, *p1, k2, yf, sl 1, k1, psso, k1, p1, k1, yfrn, p2tog, k1; rep from * to end.

2nd and every alt row: K1, yfrn, p2tog, *k2, p5, k2, yfrn, p2tog; rep from * to last st, k1.

3rd row: K1, yfrn, p2tog, k1, *p1, k1, yf, sl 1, k2tog, psso, yf, k1, p1, k1, yfrn, p2tog, k1; rep from * to end.

5th row: As 1st row.

7th row: K1, yfrn, p2tog, k1, *p1, k5, p1, k1, yfrn, p2tog, k1; rep from * to end.

8th row: As 2nd row.

Rep these 8 rows.

Twist Cable and Ladder Lace

Multiple of 7 + 6.

1st row (right side): K1, *k2tog, [yf] twice, sl 1, k1, psso, k3; rep from * to last 5 sts, k2tog, [yf] twice, sl 1, k1, psso, k1.

2nd row: K2, *[KB1, k1] into double yf of previous row, k1, p3, k1; rep from * to last 4 sts, [KB1, k1] into double yf of previous row, k2.

3rd row: K1, *k2tog, [yf] twice, sl 1, k1, psso, knit into 3rd st on left-hand needle, then knit into 2nd st, then knit into 1st st, slipping all 3 sts onto right-hand needle tog; rep from * to last 5 sts, k2tog, [yf] twice, sl 1, k1, psso, k1.

4th row: As 2nd row.

Rep these 4 rows.

Fish Scale Lace Panel

Worked over 17 sts on a background of St st.

1st row (right side): K1, yf, k3, sl 1, k1, psso, p5, k2tog, k3, yf, k1.

2nd row: P6, k5, p6.

3rd row: K2, yf, k3, sl 1, k1, psso, p3, k2tog, k3, yf, k2.

4th row: P7, k3, p7.

5th row: K3, yf, k3, sl 1, k1, psso, p1, k2tog, k3, yf, k3.

6th row: P8, k1, p8.

7th row: K4, yf, k3, sl 1, k2tog, psso, k3, yf, k4.

8th row: Purl.

Rep these 8 rows.

Little Shell Insertion

Worked over 7 sts on a background of St st.

1st row (right side): Knit.

2nd row: Purl.

3rd row: K1, yfrn, p1, p3tog, p1, yon, k1.

4th row: Purl.

Rep these 4 rows.

When knitting in the round, use a needle that is slightly smaller in length than the circumference of the knitted object.

Feather and Fan

Multiple of 18 + 2.

1st row (right side): Knit.

2nd row: Purl.

3rd row: K1, *[k2tog] 3 times, [yf, k1] 6 times, [k2tog] 3 times; rep from * to last st, k1.

4th row: Knit.

Rep these 4 rows.

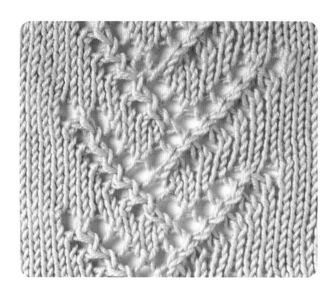

Eyelet Twigs

Worked over 14 sts on a background of St st.

1st row (right side): K1, yf, k3tog, yf, k3, yf, sl 1, k2tog, psso, yf, k4.

2nd and every alt row: Purl.

3rd row: Yf, k3tog, yf, k5, yf, sl 1, k2tog, psso, yf, k3.

5th row: K5, yf, k3tog, yf, k1, yf, sl 1, k2tog, psso, yf, k2.

7th row: K4, yf, k3tog, yf, k3, yf, sl 1, k2tog, psso, yf, k1.

9th row: K3, yf, k3tog, yf, k5, yf, sl 1, k2tog, psso, yf.

11th row: K2, yf, k3tog, yf, k1, yf, sl 1, k2tog, psso, yf, k5.

12th row: Purl.

Rep these 12 rows.

Large Lattice Lace

Multiple of 6 + 2.

1st row (right side): K1, p1, *yon, k2tog tbl, k2tog, yfrn, p2; rep from * to last 6 sts, yon, k2tog tbl, k2tog, yfrn, p1, k1.

2nd row: K2, *p4, k2; rep from * to end.

3rd row: K1, p1, *k2tog, [yf] twice, k2tog tbl, p2; rep from * to last 6 sts, k2tog, [yf] twice, k2tog tbl, p1, k1.

4th row: K2, *p1, [k1, p1] into double yf of previous row, p1, k2; rep from * to end.

5th row: K1, *k2tog, yfrn, p2, yon, k2tog tbl; rep from * to last st, k1.

6th row: K1, p2, *k2, p4; rep from * to last 5 sts, k2, p2, k1.

7th row: K1, yf, *k2tog tbl, p2, k2tog, [yf] twice; rep from * to last 7 sts, k2tog tbl, p2, k2tog, yf, k1.

8th row: K1, p2, k2, p1, *[k1, p1] into double yf of previous row, p1, k2, p1; rep from * to last 2 sts, p1, k1.

Rep these 8 rows.

Diamond and Bobble Panel

Worked over 11 sts on a background of reverse St st.

1st row (right side): P1, yon, sl 1, k1, psso, p5, k2tog, yfrn, p1.

2nd row: K2, p1, k5, p1, k2.

3rd row: P2, yon, sl 1, k1, psso, p3, k2tog, yfrn, p2.

4th row: K3, [p1, k3] twice.

5th row: P3, yon, sl 1, k1, psso, p1, k2tog, yfrn, p3.

6th row: K4, p1, k1, p1, k4.

7th row: P4, yon, sl 1, k2tog, psso, yfrn, p4.

8th row: K5, p1, k5.

9th row: P3, k2tog, yfrn, p1, yon, sl 1, k1, psso, p3.

10th row: As 4th row.

11th row: P2, k2tog, yfrn, p3, yon, sl 1, k1, psso, p2.

12th row: As 2nd row.

13th row: P1, k2tog, yfrn, p5, yon, sl 1, k1, psso, p1.

14th row: K1, p1, k7, p1, k1.

15th row: K2tog, yfrn, p3, make bobble as follows: into next st work [k1, yf, k1, yf, k1] turn, p5, turn, k5, turn, p2tog, p1, p2tog tbl, turn, sl 1, k2tog, psso, p3, yon, sl 1, k1, psso.

16th row: K1, p1, k3, KB1, k3, p1, k1.

Rep these 16 rows.

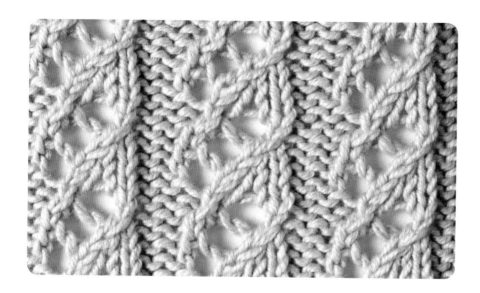

Waterfall Pattern

Multiple of 6 + 3.

1st row (right side): P3, *k3, yo, p3; rep from * to end.

2nd row: K3, *p4, k3; rep from * to end.

3rd row: P3, *k1, k2tog, yo, k1, p3; rep from * to end.

4th row: K3, *p2, p2tog, k3; rep from * to end.

5th row: P3, *k1, yo, k2tog, p3; rep from * to end.

6th row: K3, *p3, k3; rep from * to end.

Rep these 6 rows.

Alternating Lace

Multiple of 6 + 5.

1st row (right side): K1, *yf, sl 1, k2tog, psso, yf, k3; rep from * to last 4 sts, yf, sl 1, k2tog, psso, yf, k1.

2nd row: Purl.

Rep the last 2 rows 3 times more.

9th row: K4, *yf, sl 1, k2tog, psso, yf, k3; rep from * to last st, k1.

10th row: Purl.

Rep the last 2 rows 3 times more.

Rep these 16 rows.

Zigzag Insertion

Worked over 5 sts on a background of reverse St st.

1st row: Knit.

2nd and every alt row: Purl.

3rd row: K1, k2tog, yf, k2.

5th row: K2tog, yf, k3.

7th row: Knit.

9th row: K2, yf, sl 1, k1, psso, k1.

11th row: K3, yf, sl 1, k1, psso.

12th row: Purl.

Rep these 12 rows.

Eyelet Twigs and Bobbles

Worked over 16 sts on a background of St st.

1st row (right side): K2, yf, k3tog, yf, k3, yf, sl 1, k2tog, psso, yf, k5.

2nd and every alt row: Purl.

3rd row: K1, yf, k3tog, yf, k5, yf, sl 1, k2tog, psso, yf, k4.

5th row: MB, k5, yf, k3tog, yf, k1, yf, sl 1, k2tog, psso, yf, k3.

7th row: K5, yf, k3tog, yf, k3, yf, sl 1, k2tog, psso, yf, k2.

9th row: K4, yf, k3tog, yf, k5, yf, sl 1, k2tog, psso, yf, MB.

11th row: K3, yf, k3tog, yf, k1, yf, sl 1, k2tog, psso, yf, k6.

12th row: Purl.

Rep these 12 rows.

Ears of Corn

Multiple of 12 + 2.

1st row (right side): Knit.

2nd row: Purl.

3rd row: K4, k2tog, k1, yf, *k9, k2tog, k1, yf; rep from * to last 7 sts, k7.

4th row: P8, yrn, p1, p2tog, *p9, yrn, p1, p2tog; rep from * to last 3 sts, p3.

5th row: K2, *k2tog, k1, yf, k9; rep from * to end.

6th row: P10, yrn, p1, p2tog, *p9, yrn, p1, p2tog; rep from * to last st, p1.

Work 2 rows in St st, starting knit.

9th row: K7, yf, k1, sl 1, k1, psso, *k9, yf, k1, sl 1, k1, psso; rep from * to last 4 sts, k4.

10th row: P3, p2tog tbl, p1, yrn, *p9, p2tog tbl, p1, yrn; rep from * to last 8 sts, p8.

11th row: *K9, yf, k1, sl 1, k1, psso; rep from * to last 2 sts, k2.

12th row: P1, p2tog tbl, p1, yrn, *p9, p2tog tbl, p1, yrn; rep from * to last 10 sts, p10.

Rep these 12 rows.

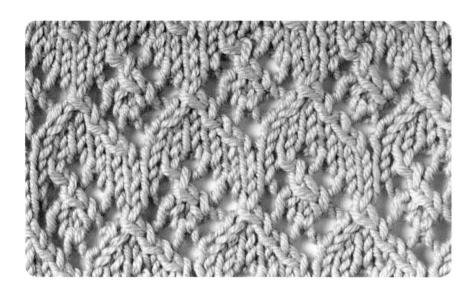

Diamond Lace II

Multiple of 6 + 3.

1st row (right side): *K4, yf, sl 1, k1, psso; rep from * to last 3 sts, k3.

2nd and every alt row: Purl.

3rd row: K2, *k2tog, yf, k1, yf, sl 1, k1, psso, k1; rep from * to last st, k1.

5th row: K1, k2tog, yf, *k3, yf, sl 1, k2tog, psso, yf; rep from * to last 6 sts, k3, yf, sl 1, k1, psso, k1.

7th row: K3, *yf, sl 1, k2tog, psso, yf, k3; rep from * to end.

9th row: As 1st row.

11th row: K1, *yf, sl 1, k1, psso, k4; rep from * to last 2 sts, yf, sl 1, k1, psso.

13th row: K2, *yf, sl 1, k1, psso, k1, k2tog, yf, k1; rep from * to last st, k1.

15th row: As 7th row.

17th row: As 5th row.

19th row: As 11th row.

20th row: Purl.

Rep these 20 rows.

Eyelet Lattice Insertion

Worked over 8 sts on a background of St st.

1st row (right side): K1, [k2tog, yf] 3 times, k1.

2nd row: Purl.

3rd row: K2, [k2tog, yf] twice, k2.

4th row: Purl.

Rep these 4 rows.

Take the time to learn how to read knitting charts; it'll make your knitting that much easier.

Braided Lace Panel

Worked over 20 sts on a background of St st.

1st and every alt row (wrong side): Purl.

2nd row: K4, [yf, sl 1, k1, psso] twice, k3, [k2tog, yf] twice, k5.

4th row: K2, [k2tog, yf] twice, k4, [k2tog, yf] twice, k1, yf, sl 1, k1, psso, k3.

6th row: K1, [k2tog, yf] twice, k4, [k2tog, yf] twice, k1, [yf, sl 1, k1, psso] twice, k2.

8th row: [K2tog, yf] twice, k4, [k2tog, yf] twice, k3, [yf, sl 1, k1, psso] twice, k1.

10th row: K2, [yf, sl 1, k1, psso] twice, k1, [k2tog, yf] twice, k5, [yf, sl 1, k1, psso] twice.

12th row: K3, yf, sl 1, k1, psso, yf, sl 1, k2tog, psso, yf, k2tog, yf, k4, [k2tog, yf] twice, k2.

14th row: K4, yf, sl 1, k1, psso, yf, sl 1, k2tog, psso, yf, k4, [k2tog, yf] twice, k3.

16th row: K5, [yf, sl 1, k1, psso] twice, k3, [k2tog, yf] twice, k4.

18th row: K3, k2tog, yf, k1, [yf, sl 1, k1, psso] twice, k4, [yf, sl 1, k1, psso] twice, k2.

20th row: K2, [k2tog, yf] twice, k1, [yf, sl 1, k1, psso] twice, k4, [yf, sl 1, k1, psso] twice, k1.

22nd row: K1, [k2tog, yf] twice, k3, [yf, sl 1, k1, psso] twice, k4, [yf, sl 1, k1, psso] twice.

24th row: [K2tog, yf] twice, k5, [yf, sl 1, k1, psso] twice, k1, [k2tog, yf] twice, k2.

26th row: K2 [yf, sl 1, k1, psso] twice, k4, yf, sl 1, k1, psso, yf, k3tog, yf, k2tog, yf, k3.

28th row: K3, [yf, sl 1, k1, psso] twice, k4, yf, k3tog, yf, k2tog, yf, k4.

Rep these 28 rows.

Creeping Vines

Multiple of 22 + 3.

1st row (right side): K4, k2tog, k3, [yf, k2tog] twice, *yf, k13, k2tog, k3, [yf, k2tog] twice; rep from * to last 12 sts, yf, k12.

2nd and every alt row: Purl.

3rd row: K3, *k2tog, k3, yf, k1, yf, [sl 1, k1, psso, yf] twice, k3, sl 1, k1, psso, k7; rep from * to end.

5th row: K2, k2tog, [k3, yf] twice, [sl 1, k1, psso, yf] twice, k3, sl 1, k1, psso, *k5, k2tog, [k3, yf] twice, [sl 1, k1, psso, yf] twice, k3, sl 1, k1, psso; rep from * to last 6 sts, k6.

7th row: K1, k2tog, k3, yf, k5, yf, [sl 1, k1, psso, yf] twice, k3, sl 1, k1, psso, *k3, k2tog, k3, yf, k5, yf, [sl 1, k1, psso, yf] twice, k3, sl 1, k1, psso; rep from * to last 5 sts, k5.

9th row: K12, yf, [sl 1, k1, psso, yf] twice, k3, sl 1, k1, psso, *k13, yf, [sl 1, k1, psso, yf] twice, k3, sl 1, k1, psso; rep from * to last 4 sts, k4.

11th row: *K7, k2tog, k3, [yf, k2tog] twice, yf, k1, yf, k3, sl 1, k1, psso; rep from * to last 3 sts, k3.

13th row: K6, k2tog, k3, [yf, k2tog] twice, [yf, k3] twice, sl 1, k1, psso, *k5, k2tog, k3, [yf, k2tog] twice, [yf, k3] twice, sl 1, k1, psso; rep from * to last 2 sts, k2.

15th row: K5, k2tog, k3, [yf, k2tog] twice, yf, k5, yf, k3, sl 1, k1, psso, *k3, k2tog, k3, [yf, k2tog] twice, yf, k5, yf, k3, sl 1, k1, psso; rep from * to last st, k1.

16th row: Purl.

Rep these 16 rows.

Lacy Chain

Worked over 16 sts on a background of St st.

1st row (right side): K5, yf, sl 1, k1, psso, k2, yf, sl 1, k1, psso, k5.

2nd and every alt row: Purl.

3rd row: K3, k2tog, yf, k1, yf, sl 1, k1, psso, k2, yf, sl 1, k1, psso, k4.

5th row: K2, k2tog, yf, k3, yf, sl 1, k1, psso, k2, yf, sl 1, k1, psso, k3.

7th row: K1, k2tog, yf, k2, k2tog, yf, k1, yf, sl 1, k1, psso, k2, yf, sl 1, k1, psso, k2.

9th row: K2tog, yf, k2, k2tog, yf, k3, yf, sl 1, k1, psso, k2, yf, sl 1, k1, psso, k1.

11th row: K2, yf, sl 1, k1, psso, k2, yf, sl 1, k1, psso, yf, k2tog, yf, k2, k2tog, yf, k2tog.

13th row: K3, yf, sl 1, k1, psso, k2, yf, sl 1, k2tog, psso, yf, k2, k2tog, yf, k2.

15th row: K4, yf, sl 1, k1, psso, k2, yf, sl 1, k1, psso, k1, k2tog, yf, k3.

16th row: Purl.

Rep these 16 rows.

Moss Lace Diamonds

Multiple of 8 + 1.

1st row (right side): K1, *p1, k1; rep from * to end.

2nd row: K1, *p1, K1; rep from * to end.

Rep the last 2 rows once more.

5th row: K1, *yf, sl 1, k1, psso, k3, k2tog, yf, k1; rep from * to end.

6th row: Purl.

7th row: K2, *yf, sl 1, k1, psso, k1, k2tog, yf, k3; rep from * to last 7 sts, yf, sl 1, k1, psso, k1, k2tog, yf, k2.

8th row: Purl.

9th row: K3, *yf, sl 1, k2tog, psso, yf, k5; rep from * to last 6 sts, yf, sl 1, k2tog, psso, yf, k3.

10th row: Purl.

11th row: K1, *p1, k1; rep from * to end.

Rep the last row 3 times more.

Rep these 14 rows.

Lace Check

Multiple of 18 + 9.

1st row (wrong side): Purl.

2nd row: K1, *[yf, k2tog] 4 times, k10; rep from * to last 8 sts, [yf, k2tog] 4 times.

3rd row: Purl.

4th row: *[Sl 1, k1, psso, yf] 4 times, k10; rep from * to last 9 sts, [sl 1, k1, psso, yf] 4 times, k1.

Rep the last 4 rows twice more.

13th row: Purl.

14th row: *K10, [yf, k2tog] 4 times; rep from * to last 9 sts, k9.

15th row: Purl.

16th row: K9, *[sl 1, k1, psso, yf] 4 times, k10; rep from * to end.

Rep the last 4 rows twice more.

Rep these 24 rows.

Zigzag Panel

Worked over 9 sts on a background of St st.

1st row (right side): K3, sl 1, k1, psso, yf, k2tog, yf, k2.

2nd and every alt row: Purl.

3rd row: K2, sl 1, k1, psso, yf, k2tog, yf, k3.

5th row: K1, sl 1, k1, psso, yf, k2tog, yf, k4.

7th row: Sl 1, k1, psso, yf, k2tog, yf, k5.

9th row: K2, yf, sl 1, k1, psso, yf, k2tog, k3.

11th row: K3, yf, sl 1, k1, psso, yf, k2tog, k2.

13th row: K4, yf, sl 1, k1, psso, yf, k2tog, k1.

15th row: K5, yf, sl 1, k1, psso, yf, k2tog.

16th row: Purl.

Rep these 16 rows.

Horseshoe Print

Multiple of 10 + 1.

1st row (wrong side): Purl.

2nd row: K1, *yf, k3, sl 1, k2tog, psso, k3, yf, k1; rep from * to end.

3rd row: Purl.

4th row: P1, *k1, yf, k2, sl 1, k2tog, psso, k2, yf, k1, p1; rep from * to end.

5th row: K1, *p9, k1; rep from * to end.

6th row: P1, *k2, yf, k1, sl 1, k2tog, psso, k1, yf, k2, p1; rep from * to end.

7th row: As 5th row.

8th row: P1, *k3, yf, sl 1, k2tog, psso, yf, k3, p1; rep from * to end.

Rep these 8 rows.

Stitch markers are your friends. Count the stitches on your needle within each section of the pattern when you reach each marker.

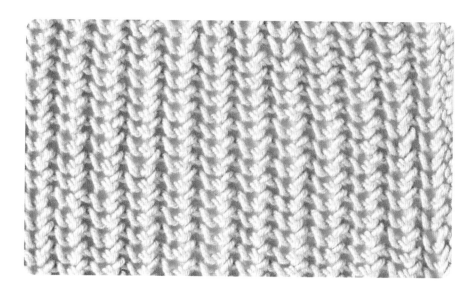

Purse Stitch

Multiple of 2.

1st row: P1, *yrn, p2tog; rep from * to last st, p1.

Rep this row.

Feather Openwork

Multiple of 5 + 2.

1st row (right side): K1, *k2tog, yf, k1, yf, sl 1, k1, psso; rep from * to last st, k1.

2nd row: Purl.

Rep these 2 rows.

Single Lace Rib

Multiple of 4 + 1.

1st row (right side): K1, *yf, k2tog, p1, k1; rep from * to end.

2nd row: P1, *yrn, p2tog, k1, p1; rep from * to end.

Rep these 2 rows.

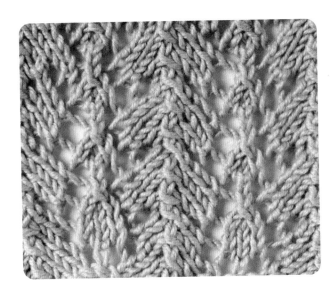

Fancy Horseshoe Print

Multiple of 10 + 1.

1st row (right side): K1, *yf, k3, sl 1, k2tog, psso, k3, yf, k1; rep from * to end.

2nd and 4th rows: Purl.

3rd row: K2, yf, k2, sl 1, k2tog, psso, k2, *yf, k3, yf, k2, sl 1, k2tog, psso, k2; rep from * to last 2 sts, yf, k2.

5th row: K2tog, [yf, k1] twice, *sl 1, k2tog, psso, [k1, yf] twice, sl 1, k2tog, psso, [yf, k1] twice; rep from * to last 7 sts, sl 1, k2tog, psso, [k1, yf] twice, sl 1, k1, psso.

6th row: Purl.

Rep these 6 rows.

Scallop Pattern

Multiple of 13 + 2.

Note: Sts should only be counted after the 5th and 6th rows.

1st row (right side): K1, *sl 1, k1, psso, k9, k2tog; rep from * to last st, k1.

2nd row: Purl.

3rd row: K1, *sl 1, k1, psso, k7, k2tog; rep from * to last st, k1.

4th row: Purl.

5th row: K1, *sl 1, k1, psso, yf, [k1, yf] 5 times, k2tog; rep from * to last st, k1.

6th row: Knit.

Rep these 6 rows.

Simple Garter Stitch Lace

Multiple of 4 + 2.

1st row: K2, *yfrn, p2tog, k2; rep from * to end.

Rep this row.

A magnetic needlepoint board or post-it help you to keep track of the row on which you're working.

Zigzag Panel with Diamonds

Worked over 9 sts on a background of St st.

1st row (right side): K2, yf, sl 1, k1, psso, k5.

2nd and every alt row: Purl.

3rd row: K3, yf, sl 1, k1, psso, k4.

5th row: K4, yf, sl 1, k1, psso, k3.

7th row: K5, yf, sl 1, k1, psso, k2.

9th row: K2, yf, sl 1, k1, psso, k2, yf, sl 1, k1, psso, k1.

11th row: K1, [yf, sl 1, k1, psso] twice, k2, yf, sl 1, k1, psso.

13th row: K2, yf, sl 1, k1, psso, k2, k2tog, yf, k1.

15th row: K5, k2tog, yf, k2.

17th row: K4, k2tog, yf, k3.

19th row: K3, k2tog, yf, k4.

21st row: K2, k2tog, yf, k5.

23rd row: K1, k2tog, yf, k3, yf, sl 1, k1, psso, k1.

25th row: K2tog, yf, k3, [yf, sl 1, k1, psso] twice.

27th row: K1, yf, sl 1, k1, psso, k3, yf, sl 1, k1, psso, k1.

28th row: Purl.

Rep these 28 rows.

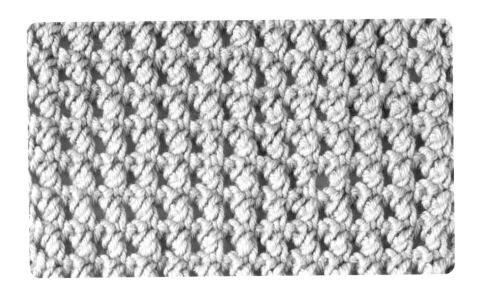

Ridged Openwork

Multiple of 2 + 1.

Note: Sts should only be counted after the 1st, 3rd or 4th rows.

1st row (right side): Purl.

2nd row: *P2tog; rep from * to last st, p1.

3rd row: P1, *purl through horizontal strand of yarn lying between stitch just worked and next st, p1; rep from * to end.

4th row: P1, *yrn, p2tog; rep from * to end.

Rep these 4 rows.

Wave Pattern

Multiple of 14 + 3.

1st row (right side): K2, yf, k5, k3tog, k5, yf, *k1, yf, k5, k3tog, k5, yf; rep from * to last 2 sts, k2.

2nd row: Purl.

3rd row: Knit.

4th row: As 1st row.

Rep the last 4 rows once more, then the first 3 rows again.

12th, 13th, and 15th rows: Purl.

14th and 16th rows: Knit.

Rep these 16 rows.

Chevron and Feather

Multiple of 13 + 1.

1st row (right side): *K1, yf, k4, k2tog, sl 1, k1, psso, k4, yf; rep from * to last st, k1.

2nd row: Purl.

Rep these 2 rows.

Astrakhan Bobbles

Multiple of 12 + 3.

Either side of this stitch may be used.

1st row: K2, *yf, k4, p3tog, k4, yf, k1; rep from * to last st, k1.

Rep this row 5 times more.

7th row: K1, p2tog, *k4, yf, k1, yf, k4, p3tog; rep from * to last 12 sts, k4, yf, k1, yf, k4, p2tog, k1.

Rep this row 5 times more.

Rep these 12 rows.

Eyelet Fan Panel

Worked over 13 sts on a background of St st.

Work 4 rows in garter st (1st row is right side).

5th row: Sl 1, k1, psso, k4, yf, k1, yf, k4, k2tog.

6th, 8th, 10th, and 12th rows: Purl.

7th row: Sl 1, k1, psso, [k3, yf] twice, k3, k2tog.

9th row: Sl 1, k1, psso, k2, yf, k2tog, yf, k1, yf, sl 1, k1, psso, yf, k2, k2tog.

11th row: Sl 1, k1, psso, k1, yf, k2tog, yf, k3, yf, sl 1, k1, psso, yf, k1, k2tog.

13th row: Sl 1, k1, psso, [yf, k2tog] twice, yf, k1, [yf, sl 1, k1, psso] twice, yf, k2tog.

14th row: Purl.

Rep these 14 rows.

Flickering Flames

Multiple of 10 + 1.

1st row (right side): K1, *yf, k3, sl 1, k2tog, psso, k3, yf, k1; rep from * to end.

2nd row: Purl.

Rep the last 2 rows 3 times more.

9th row: K2tog, k3, yf, k1, yf, k3, *sl 1, k2tog, psso, k3, yf, k1, yf, k3; rep from * to last 2 sts, sl 1, k1, psso.

10th row: Purl.

Rep the last 2 rows 3 times more.

Rep these 16 rows.

Gate and Ladder Pattern

Multiple of 9 + 3.

Foundation row (wrong side): Purl.

1st row: K1, k2tog, k3, [yf] twice, k3, *k3tog, k3, [yf] twice, k3; rep from * to last 3 sts, k2tog, k1.

2nd row: P6, k1, *p8, k1; rep from * to last 5 sts, p5.

Rep the last 2 rows.

If you're working from a book or magazine, try photocopying your pattern. It's convenient for knitting on the go.

Wavy Eyelet Rib

Multiple of 7 + 2.

1st row (right side): *P2, yon, sl 1, k1, psso, k1, k2tog, yfrn; rep from * to last 2 sts, p2.

2nd row: K2, *p5, k2; rep from * to end.

Rep the last 2 rows twice more.

7th row: *P2, k5; rep from * to last 2 sts, p2.

8th row: As 2nd row.

9th row: *P2, k2tog, yf, k1, yf, sl 1, k1, psso; rep from * to last 2 sts, p2.

10th row: As 2nd row.

Rep the last 2 rows twice more.

15th row: As 7th row.

16th row: As 2nd row.

Rep these 16 rows.

Fish-Scale Pattern

Multiple of 12.

1st row (right side): *Sl 1, k1, psso, k3, yfrn, p2, yon, k3, k2tog; rep from * to end.

2nd row: *P2tog, p2, yon, k4, yfrn, p2, p2tog tbl; rep from * to end.

3rd row: *Sl 1, k1, psso, k1, yfrn, p6, yon, k1, k2tog; rep from * to end.

4th row: *P2tog, yon, k8, yfrn, p2tog tbl; rep from * to end.

5th row: P1, yon, k3, k2tog, sl 1, k1, psso, k3, yfrn, *p2, yon, k3, k2tog, sl 1, k1, psso, k3, yfrn; rep from * to last st, p1.

6th row: K2, yfrn, p2, p2tog tbl, p2tog, p2, yon, *k4, yfrn, p2, p2tog tbl, p2tog, p2, yon; rep from * to last 2 sts, k2.

7th row: P3, yon, k1, k2tog, sl 1, k1, psso, k1, yfrn, *p6, yon, k1, k2tog, sl 1, k1, psso, k1, yfrn; rep from * to last 3 sts, p3.

8th row: K4, yfrn, p2tog tbl, p2tog, yon, *k8, yfrn, p2tog tbl, p2tog, yon; rep from * to last 4 sts, k4.

Rep these 8 rows.

Lyre Panel

Worked over 21 sts on a background of St st.

1st and every alt row (wrong side): Purl.

2nd row: K1, yf, k2tog, k5, k2tog, yf, k1, yf, sl 1, k1, psso, k5, sl 1, k1, psso, yf, k1.

4th row: K1, yf, k2tog, k4, k2tog, yf, k3, yf, sl 1, k1, psso, k4, sl 1, k1, psso, yf, k1.

6th row: K1, yf, k2tog, k3, k2tog, yf, k5, yf, sl 1, k1, psso, k3, sl 1, k1, psso, yf, k1.

8th row: K1, yf, k2tog, k2, [k2tog, yf] twice, k3, [yf, sl 1, k1, psso] twice, k2, sl 1, k1, psso, yf, k1.

10th, 12th, 14th, 16th, and 18th rows: K1, yf, k2tog, k3, yf, k2tog, yf, sl 1, k1, psso, k1, k2tog, yf, sl 1, k1, psso, yf, k3, sl 1, k1, psso, yf, k1.

20th row: K1, yf, k2tog, k1, k2tog, yf, k9, yf, sl 1, k1, psso, k1, sl 1, k1, psso, yf, k1.

Rep these 20 rows.

Lacy Openwork

Multiple of 4 + 1.

1st row: K1, *yfrn, p3tog, yon, k1; rep from * to end.

2nd row: P2tog, yon, k1, yfrn, *p3tog, yon, k1, yfrn; rep from * to last 2 sts, p2tog.

Rep these 2 rows.

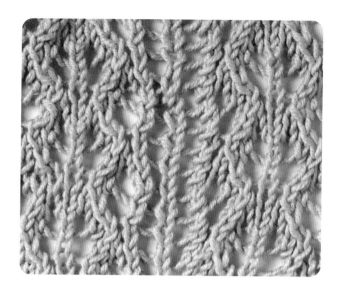

Tracery Pattern

Multiple of 12 + 1.

1st row (right side): K1, *yf, k2tog, yf, sl 1, k1, psso, k3, k2tog, yf, k3; rep from * to end.

2nd and every alt row: P1, *yrn, p2tog, p10; rep from * to end.

3rd row: K1, *yf, k2tog, yf, k1, sl 1, k1, psso, k1, k2tog, k1, yf, k3; rep from * to end.

5th row: K1, *yf, k2tog, k1, k2tog, yf, k1, yf, sl 1, k1, psso, k4; rep from * to end.

7th row: K1, *yf, [k2tog] twice, k1, [yf, k1] twice, sl 1, k1, psso, k3; rep from * to end.

8th row: As 2nd row.

Rep these 8 rows.

Loose Lattice Lace

Multiple of 8 + 3.

Note: Sts should only be counted after the 5th, 6th, 11th, and 12th rows.

1st row (right side): K1, *k2tog, k1, yf, k1, sl 1, k1, psso, k2; rep from * to last 2 sts, k2.

2nd and every alt row: Purl.

3rd row: *K2tog, k1, [yf, k1] twice, sl 1, k1, psso; rep from * to last 3 sts, k3.

5th row: K2, *yf, k3, yf, k1, sl 1, k1, psso, k1; rep from * to last st, k1.

7th row: K4, *k2tog, k1, yf, k1, sl 1, k1, psso, k2; rep from * to last 7 sts, k2tog, k1, yf, k1, sl 1, k1, psso, k1.

9th row: K3, *k2tog, k1, [yf, k1] twice, sl 1, k1, psso; rep from * to end.

11th row: K2, *k2tog, k1, yf, k3, yf, k1; rep from * to last st, k1.

12th row: Purl.

Rep these 12 rows.

Pyramid Panel

Worked over 17 sts on a background of St st.

1st row (right side): [K1, yf, sl 1, k1, psso] twice, p5, [k2tog, yf, k1] twice.

2nd row: P6, k5, p6.

3rd row: K2, yf, sl 1, k1, psso, k1, yf, sl 1, k1, psso, p3, k2tog, yf, k1, k2tog, yf, k2.

4th row: P7, k3, p7.

5th row: K3, yf, sl 1, k1, psso, k1, yf, sl 1, k1, psso, p1, k2tog, yf, k1, k2tog, yf, k3.

6th row: P8, k1, p8.

7th row: K4, yf, sl 1, k1, psso, k1, yf, sl 1, k2tog, psso, yf, k1, k2tog, yf, k4.

8th and every alt row: Purl.

9th row: K5, yf, sl 1, k1, psso, k3, k2tog, yf, k5.

11th row: K6, yf, sl 1, k1, psso, k1, k2tog, yf, k6.

13th row: K7, yf, sl 1, k2tog, psso, yf, k7.

14th row: Purl.

Rep these 14 rows.

Lacy Zigzag

Multiple of 6 + 1.

1st row (right side): *Sl 1, k1, psso, k2, yf, k2; rep from * to last st, k1.

2nd row: Purl.

Rep the last 2 rows twice more.

7th row: K3, *yf, k2, k2tog, k2; rep from * to last 4 sts, yf, k2, k2tog.

8th row: Purl.

Rep the last 2 rows twice more.

Rep these 12 rows.

Lace Loops

Worked over 20 sts on a background of St st.

1st row and every alt row (wrong side): Purl.

2nd row: K2, yf, sl 1, k1, psso, k1, k2tog, yf, k1, yf, sl 1, k1, psso, k10.

4th row: K3, yf, sl 1, k2tog, psso, yf, k3, yf, sl 1, k1, psso, k3, k2tog, yf, k4.

6th row: K4, yf, sl 1, k1, psso, k4, yf, sl 1, k1, psso, k1, k2tog, yf, k1, yf, sl 1, k1, psso, k2.

8th row: K11, yf, k3tog, yf, k3, yf, sl 1, k1, psso, k1.

10th row: K11, k2tog, yf, k5, yf, sl 1, k1, psso.

12th row: K10, k2tog, yf, k1, yf, sl 1, k1, psso, k1, k2tog, yf, k2.

14th row: K4, yf, sl 1, k1, psso, k3, k2tog, yf, k3, yf, k3tog, yf, k3.

16th row: K2, k2tog, yf, k1, yf, sl 1, k1, psso, k1, k2tog, yf, k4, k2tog, yf, k4.

18th row: K1, k2tog, yf, k3, yf, sl 1, k2tog, yf, k11.

20th row: K2tog, yf, k5, yf, sl 1, k1, psso, k11.

Rep these 20 rows.

Fir Cone

Multiple of 10 + 1.

1st row (wrong side): Purl.

2nd row: K1, *yf, k3, sl 1, k2tog, psso, k3, yf, k1; rep from * to end.

Rep the last 2 rows 3 times more.

9th row: Purl.

10th row: K2tog, *k3, yf, k1, yf, k3, sl 1, k2tog, psso; rep from * to last 9 sts, k3, yf, k1, yf, k3, sl 1, k1, psso.

Rep the last 2 rows 3 times more.

Rep these 16 rows.

Chalice Pattern

Multiple of 10 + 3.

1st row (right side): K2, yf, k1, sl 1, k1, psso, k3, k2tog, k1, *[yf, k1] twice, sl 1, k1, psso, k3, k2tog, k1; rep from * to last 2 sts, yf, k2.

2nd and every alt row: Purl.

3rd row: K3, *yf, k1, sl 1, k1, psso, k1, k2tog, k1, yf, k3; rep from * to end.

5th row: K4, yf, k1, sl 1, k2tog, psso, k1, yf, *k5, yf, k1, sl 1, k2tog, psso, k1, yf; rep from * to last 4 sts, k4.

7th row: K2, k2tog, k1, yf, k3, yf, k1, sl 1, k1, psso, *k1, k2tog, k1, yf, k3, yf, k1, sl 1, k1, psso; rep from * to last 2 sts, k2.

9th row: K1, sl 1, k1, psso, k2, yf, k3, yf, k2, *sl 1, k2tog, psso, k2, yf, k3, yf, k2; rep from * to last 3 sts, k2tog, k1.

11th row: K3, *k2tog, k1, [yf, k1] twice, sl 1, k1, psso, k3; rep from * to end.

13th row: K2, k2tog, k1, yf, k3, yf, k1, sl 1, k1, psso, *k1, k2tog, k1, yf, k3, yf, k1, sl 1, k1, psso; rep from * to last 2 sts, k2.

15th row: K1, sl 1, k1, psso, k1, yf, k5, yf, k1, *sl 1, k2tog, psso, k1, yf, k5, yf, k1; rep from * to last 3 sts, k2tog, k1.

17th row: K3, *yf, k1, sl 1, k1, psso, k1, k2tog, k1, yf, k3; rep from * to end.

19th row: K3, *yf, k2, sl 1, k2tog, psso, k2, yf, k3; rep from * to end.

20th row: Purl.

Rep these 20 rows.

Comb Panel

Worked over 8 sts on a background of reverse St st.

1st row (wrong side): K1, p6, k1.

2nd row: P1, yb, sl 1, k1, psso, k4, yfrn, p1.

3rd row: K1, p1, yrn, p3, p2tog tbl, k1.

4th row: P1, yb, sl 1, k1, psso, k2, yf, k2, p1.

5th row: K1, p3, yrn, p1, p2tog tbl, k1.

6th row: P1, yb, sl 1, k1, psso, yf, k4, p1.

7th row: As 1st row.

8th row: P1, yon, k4, k2tog, p1.

9th row: K1, p2tog, p3, yrn, p1, k1.

10th row: P1, k2, yf, k2, k2tog, p1.

11th row: K1, p2tog, p1, yrn, p3, k1.

12th row: P1, k4, yf, k2tog, p1.

Rep these 12 rows.

Alternating Feather Openwork

Multiple of 6 + 1.

1st row (right side): K1, *k2tog, yf, k1, yf, sl 1, k1, psso, k1; rep from * to end.

2nd row: Purl.

Rep these 2 rows 5 times more.

13th row: K1, *yf, sl 1, k1, psso, k1, k2tog, yf, k1; rep from * to end.

14th row: Purl.

Rep the last 2 rows 5 times more.

Rep these 24 rows.

Staggered Eyelets

Multiple of 4 + 3.

Work 2 rows in St st, starting knit.

3rd row (right side): *K2, k2tog, yf; rep from * to last 3 sts, k3.

Work 3 rows in st st, starting purl.

7th row: *K2tog, yf, k2; rep from * to last 3 sts, k2tog, yf, k1.

8th row: Purl.

Rep these 8 rows.

If you need to join a new ball of yarn, do it at the end of a row where you can more easily hide the ends in the border.

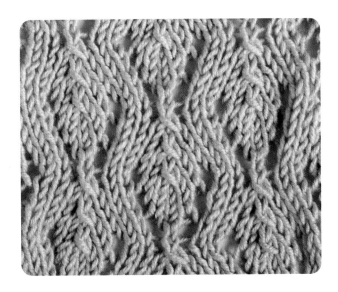

Clover Pattern

Multiple of 12 + 1.

1st row (right side): K2tog, k4, yf, k1, yf, k4, *sl 1, k2tog, psso, k4, yf, k1, yf, k4; rep from * to last 2 sts, sl 1, k1, psso.

2nd and every alt row: Purl.

3rd row: K2tog, k3, [yf, k3] twice, *sl 1, k2tog, psso, k3, [yf, k3] twice; rep from * to last 2 sts, sl 1, k1, psso.

5th row: K2tog, k2, yf, k5, yf, k2, *sl 1, k2tog, psso, k2, yf, k5, yf, k2; rep from * to last 2 sts, sl 1, k1, psso.

7th row: K1, *yf, k4, sl 1, k2tog, psso, k4, yf, k1; rep from * to end.

9th row: K2, yf, k3, sl 1, k2tog, psso, k3, *[yf, k3] twice, sl 1, k2tog, psso, k3; rep from * to last 2 sts, yf, k2.

11th row: K3, yf, k2, sl 1, k2tog, psso, k2, *yf, k5, yf, k2, sl 1, k2tog, psso, k2; rep from * to last 3 sts, yf, k3.

12th row: Purl.

Rep these 12 rows.

Frost Flower Panel

Worked over 18 sts on a background of reverse st st.

1st row (right side): K1, yf, k3, sl 1, k1, psso, k6, k2tog, k3, yf, k1.

2nd row: P1, yrn, p4, p2tog, p4, p2tog tbl, p4, yrn, p1.

3rd row: K2, yf, k4, sl 1, k1, psso, k2, k2tog, k4, yf, k2.

4th row: P3, yrn, p4, p2tog, p2tog tbl, p4, yrn, p3.

5th through 12th rows: Rep first 4 rows twice.

13th row: P3, [k2, yf, sl 1, k1, psso] 3 times, p3.

14th row: K3, [p2, yrn, p2tog] 3 times, k3.

15th through 24th rows: Rep 13th and 14th rows 5 times.

Rep these 24 rows.

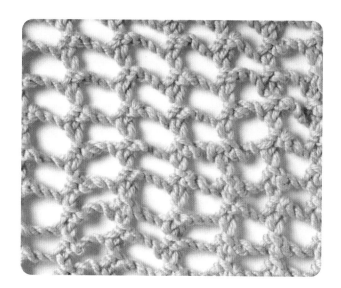

Filet Net

Multiple of 3.

1st row (right side): K2, *sl 2, pass 1st slipped st over 2nd and off needle, sl 1, pass 2nd slipped st over 3rd and off needle, slip the 3rd slipped st back onto left-hand needle, [yf] twice (to make 2 sts), knit the 3rd slipped st in usual way; rep from * to last st, k1 (original number of sts retained).

2nd row: K3, *p1, k2; rep from * to end.

Rep these 2 rows.

Arrowhead Lace

Multiple of 10 + 1.

1st row (right side): K1, *[yf, sl 1, k1, psso] twice, k1, [k2tog, yf] twice, k1; rep from * to end.

2nd row: Purl.

3rd row: K2, *yf, sl 1, k1, psso, yf, sl 1, k2tog, psso, yf, k2tog, yf, k3; rep from * to last 9 sts, yf, sl 1, k1, psso, yf, sl 1, k2tog, psso, yf, k2tog, yf, k2.

4th row: Purl.

Rep these 4 rows.

Goblet Lace

Multiple of 10 + 1.

1st row (right side): K1, *yf, sl 1, k1, psso, k2tog, yf, k1; rep from * to end.

2nd and every alt row: Purl.

Rep the last 2 rows twice more.

7th row: K1, *yf, sl 1, k1, psso, k5, k2tog, yf, k1; rep from * to end.

9th row: K2, yf, sl 1, k1, psso, k3, k2tog, yf, *k3, yf, sl 1, k1, psso, k3, k2tog, yf; rep from * to last 2 sts, k2.

11th row: K3, yf, sl 1, k1, psso, k1, k2tog, yf, *k5, yf, sl 1, k1, psso, k1, k2tog, yf; rep from * to last 3 sts, k3.

13th row: K4, yf, sl 1, k2tog, psso, yf, *k7, yf, sl 1, k2tog, psso, yf; rep from * to last 4 sts, k4.

14th row: Purl.

Rep these 14 rows

Moss Stitch Diamond Panel

Worked over 19 sts on a background of St st.

1st row (right side): K8, yf, sl 1, k2tog, psso, yf, k8.

2nd, 4th, 6th, and 8th rows: Purl.

3rd row: K7, k2tog, yf, k1, yf, sl 1, k1, psso, k7.

5th row: K6, k2tog, yf, k3, yf, sl 1, k1, psso, k6.

7th row: K5, k2tog, yf, k5, yf, sl 1, k1, psso, k5.

9th row: K4, k2tog, yf, k3, p1, k3, yf, sl 1, k1, psso, k4.

10th row: P9, k1, p9.

11th row: K3, k2tog, yf, k3, p1, k1, p1, k3, yf, sl 1, k1, psso, k3.

12th row: P8, k1, p1, k1, p8.

13th row: K2, k2tog, yf, k3, [p1, k1] twice, p1, k3, yf, sl 1, k1, psso, k2.

14th row: P7, [k1, p1] twice, k1, p7.

15th row: K1, k2tog, yf, k3, [p1, k1] 3 times, p1, k3, yf, sl 1, k1, psso, k1.

16th row: P6, [k1, p1] 3 times, k1, p6.

17th row: K2tog, yf, k3, [p1, k1] 4 times, p1, k3, yf, sl 1, k1, psso.

18th row: P5, [k1, p1] 4 times, k1, p5.

19th row: K2, yf, sl 1, k1, psso, k2, [p1, k1] 3 times, p1, k2, k2tog, yf, k2.

20th row: As 16th row.

21st row: K3, yf, sl 1, k1, psso, k2, [p1, k1] twice, p1, k2, k2tog, yf, k3.

22nd row: As 14th row.

23rd row: K4, yf, sl 1, k1, psso, k2, p1, k1, p1, k2, k2tog, yf, k4.

24th row: As 12th row.

25th row: K5, yf, sl 1, k1, psso, k2, p1, k2, k2tog, yf, k5.

26th row: As 10th row.

27th row: K6, yf, sl 1, k1, psso, k3, k2tog, yf, k6.

28th row: Purl.

29th row: K7, yf, sl 1, k1, psso, k1, k2tog, yf, k7.

30th row: Purl.

Rep these 30 rows.

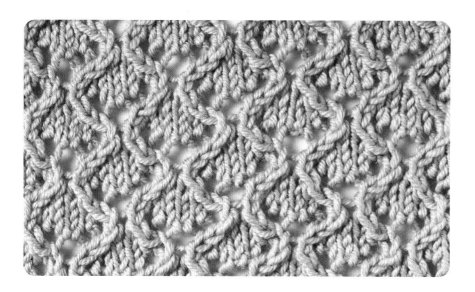

Lattice Lace

Multiple of 7 + 2.

1st row (right side): K3, *k2tog, yf, k5; rep from * to last 6 sts, k2tog, yf, k4.

2nd row: P2, *p2tog tbl, yrn, p1, yrn, p2tog, p2; rep from * to end.

3rd row: K1, *k2tog, yf, k3, yf, sl 1, k1, psso; rep from * to last st, k1.

4th row: Purl.

5th row: K1, *yf, sl 1, k1, psso, k5; rep from * to last st, k1.

6th row: *P1, yrn, p2tog, p2, p2tog tbl, yrn; rep from * to last 2 sts, p2.

7th row: *K3, yf, sl 1, k1, psso, k2tog, yf; rep from * to last 2 sts, k2.

8th row: Purl.

Rep these 8 rows.

Ribbed Diamond

Worked over 17 sts on a background of St st.

1st row (right side): K6, k2tog, yf, k1, yf, sl 1, k1, psso, k6.

2nd row: P7, k1, p1, k1, p7.

3rd row: K5, k2tog, yfrn, p1, k1, p1, yon, sl 1, k1, psso, k5.

4th row: As 2nd row.

5th row: K4, k2tog, yf, [k1, p1] twice, k1, yf, sl 1, k1, psso, k4.

6th row: P5, k1, [p1, k1] 3 times, p5.

7th row: K3, k2tog, yfrn, [p1, k1] 3 times, p1, yon, sl 1, k1, psso, k3.

8th row: As 6th row.

9th row: K2, k2tog, yf, [k1, p1] 4 times, k1, yf, sl 1, k1, psso, k2.

10th row: P3, k1, [p1, k1] 5 times, p3.

11th row: K1, k2tog, yfrn, [p1, k1] 5 times, p1, yon, sl 1, k1, psso, k1.

12th row: As 10th row.

13th row: K1, yf, sl 1, k1, psso, [p1, k1] 5 times, p1, k2tog, yf, k1.

14th row: As 10th row.

15th row: K2, yf, sl 1, k1, psso, [k1, p1] 4 times, k1, k2tog, yf, k2.

16th row: As 6th row.

17th row: K3, yf, sl 1, k1, psso, [p1, k1] 3 times, p1, k2tog, yf, k3.

18th row: As 6th row.

19th row: K4, yf, sl 1, k1, psso, [k1, p1] twice, k1, k2tog, yf, k4.

20th row: As 2nd row.

21st row: K5, yf, sl 1, k1, psso, p1, k1, p1, k2tog, yf, k5.

22nd row: As 2nd row.

23rd row: K6, yf, sl 1, k1, psso, k1, k2tog, yf, k6.

24th row: Purl.

Rep these 24 rows.

Layette Stitch

Multiple of 4 + 1.

1st row (right side): K2, *p1, k3; rep from * to last 3 sts, p1, k2.

2nd row: P2, *k1, p3; rep from * to last 3 sts, k1, p2.

3rd row: K2tog, yfrn, *p1, yon, k3tog, yfrn; rep from * to last 3 sts, p1, yon, k2tog.

4th row: K1, *p3, k1; rep from * to end.

5th row: P1, *k3, p1; rep from * to end.

6th row: As 4th row.

7th row: P1, *yon, k3tog, yfrn, p1; rep from * to end.

8th row: As 2nd row.

Rep these 8 rows.

Raised Tyre Track Panel

Worked over 10 sts on a background of St st.

1st row (right side): K4, yf, k1, sl 1, k1, psso, k3.

2nd row: P2, p2tog tbl, p1, yrn, p5.

3rd row: K6, yf, k1, sl 1, k1, psso, k1.

4th row: P2tog tbl, p1, yrn, p7.

5th row: K3, k2tog, k1, yf, k4.

6th row: P5, yrn, p1, p2tog, p2.

7th row: K1, k2tog, k1, yf, k6.

8th row: P7, yrn, p1, p2tog.

Rep these 8 rows.

Triangles and Lace

Multiple of 12 + 1.

1st row (right side): K1, *yf, sl 1, k1, psso, p7, k2tog, yf, k1; rep from * to end.

2nd row: P3, k7, *p5, k7; rep from * to last 3 sts, p3.

3rd row: K1, *yf, k1, sl 1, k1, psso, p5, k2tog, k1, yf, k1; rep from * to end.

4th row: P4, k5, *p7, k5; rep from * to last 4 sts, p4.

5th row: K1, *yf, k2, sl 1, k1, psso, p3, k2tog, k2, yf, k1; rep from * to end.

6th row: P5, k3, *p9, k3; rep from * to last 5 sts, p5.

7th row: K1, *yf, k3, sl 1, k1, psso, p1, k2tog, k3, yf, k1; rep from * to end.

8th row: P6, k1, *p11, k1; rep from * to last 6 sts, p6.

9th row: K1, *yf, k4, sl 1, k2tog, psso, k4, yf, k1; rep from * to end.

10th row: Purl.

11th row: P4, k2tog, yf, k1, yf, sl 1, k1, psso, *p7, k2tog, yf, k1, yf, sl 1, k1, psso; rep from * to last 4 sts, p4.

12th row: K4, p5, *k7, p5; rep from * to last 4 sts, k4.

13th row: P3, k2tog, k1, [yf, k1] twice, sl 1, k1, psso, *p5, k2tog, k1, [yf, k1] twice, sl 1, k1, psso; rep from * to last 3 sts, p3.

14th row: K3, p7, *k5, p7; rep from * to last 3 sts, k3.

15th row: P2, k2tog, k2, yf, k1, yf, k2, sl 1, k1, psso, *p3, k2tog, k2, yf, k1, yf, k2, sl 1, k1, psso; rep from * to last 2 sts, p2.

16th row: K2, p9, *k3, p9; rep from * to last 2 sts, k2.

17th row: P1, *k2tog, k3, yf, k1, yf, k3, sl 1, k1, psso, p1; rep from * to end.

18th row: K1, *p11, k1; rep from * to end.

19th row: K2tog, k4, yf, k1, yf, k4, *sl 1, k2tog, psso, k4, yf, k1, yf, k4; rep from * to last 2 sts, sl 1, k1, psso.

20th row: Purl.

Rep these 20 rows.

Bishop's Miter Panel

Worked over 9 sts on a background of reverse St st.

Foundation row (wrong side): K1, p1, k5, p1, k1.

1st row: P1, KB1, p2, [k1, KB1, k1, KB1, k1, KB1, k1, KB1] into next st, p2, KB1, p1.

2nd row: K1, p1, k2, p8, k2, p1, k1.

3rd row: P1, KB1, p2, k6, k2tog, p2, KB1, p1.

4th row: K1, p1, k2, p7, k2, p1, k1.

5th row: P1, KB1, p2, k5, k2tog, p2, KB1, p1.

6th row: K1, p1, k2, p6, k2, p1, k1.

7th row: P1, KB1, p2, k4, k2tog, p2, KB1, p1.

8th row: K1, p1, k2, p5, k2, p1, k1.

9th row: P1, KB1, p2, k3, k2tog, p2, KB1, p1.

10th row: K1, p1, k2, p4, k2, p1, k1.

11th row: P1, KB1, p2, k2, k2tog, p2, KB1, p1.

12th row: K1, p1, k2, p3, k2, p1, k1.

13th row: P1, KB1, p2, k1, k2tog, p2, KB1, p1.

14th row: K1, p1, k2, p2, k2, p1, k1.

15th row: P1, KB1, p2, k2tog, p2, KB1, p1.

16th row: K1, p1, [k2, p1] twice, k1.

Rep these 16 rows.

Eyelet Chevron

Multiple of 12 + 1.

1st row (right side): K4, *k2tog, yf, k1, yf, sl 1, k1, psso, k7; rep from * to last 9 sts, k2tog, yf, k1, yf, sl 1, k1, psso, k4.

2nd and every alt row: Purl.

3rd row: K3, *k2tog, yf, k3, yf, sl 1, k1, psso, k5; rep from * to last 10 sts, k2tog, yf, k3, yf, sl 1, k1, psso, k3.

5th row: K2, *k2tog, yf, k5, yf, sl 1, k1, psso, k3; rep from * to last 11 sts, k2tog, yf, k5, yf, sl 1, k1, psso, k2.

7th row: K1, *k2tog, yf, k7, yf, sl 1, k1, psso, k1; rep from * to end.

9th row: K2tog, yf, k9, *yf, sl 1, k2tog, psso, yf, k9; rep from * to last 2 sts, yf, sl 1, k1, psso.

10th row: Purl.

Rep these 10 rows.

Plumes

Multiple of 11 + 2.

1st row (right side): K1, *k2tog, k3, yf, k1, yf, k3, sl 1, k1, psso; rep from * to last st, k1.

2nd and every alt row: Purl.

3rd and 5th rows: As 1st row.

7th row: K1, *k2tog, k2, yf, k3, yf, k2, sl 1, k1, psso; rep from * to last st, k1.

9th row: K1, *k2tog, k1, yf, k5, yf, k1, sl 1, k1, psso; rep from * to last st, k1.

11th row: K1, *[k2tog, yf, k1] twice, yf, sl 1, k1, psso, k1, yf, sl 1, k1, psso; rep from * to last st, k1.

13th row: As 11th row.

15th row: As 9th row.

17th row: As 7th row.

18th row: Purl.

Rep these 18 rows.

Butterfly Panel

Worked over 15 sts on a background of reverse St st.

1st row (right side): Yb, sl 1, k1, psso, k4, yf, k3, yf, k4, k2tog.

2nd row: P2tog, p3, yrn, p5, yrn, p3, p2tog tbl.

3rd row: Yb, sl 1, k1, psso, k2, yf, k7, yf, k2, k2tog.

4th row: P2tog, p1, yrn, p9, yrn, p1, p2tog tbl.

5th row: Yb, sl 1, k1, psso, yf, k11, yf, k2tog.

6th row: P1, yrn, p4, p2tog, k1, p2tog tbl, p4, yrn, p1.

7th row: K2, yf, k3, sl 1, k1, psso, p1, k2tog, k3, yf, k2.

8th row: P3, yrn, p2, p2tog, k1, p2tog tbl, p2, yrn, p3.

9th row: K4, yf, k1, sl 1, k1, psso, p1, k2tog, k1, yf, k4.

10th row: P5, yrn, p2tog, k1, p2tog tbl, yrn, p5.

Rep these 10 rows.

Ornamental Arrow Pattern

Multiple of 12 + 1.

1st row (right side): K1, *sl 1, k1, psso, k3, yf, k1, yf, k3, k2tog, k1; rep from * to end.

2nd row: P1, *p2tog, p2, yrn, p3, yrn, p2, p2tog tbl, p1; rep from * to end.

3rd row: K1, *sl 1, k1, psso, k1, yf, k5, yf, k1, k2tog, k1; rep from * to end.

4th row: P1, *yrn, p2tog, p7, p2tog tbl, yrn, p1; rep from * to end.

5th row: K1, *yf, k3, k2tog, k1, sl 1, k1, psso, k3, yf, k1; rep from * to end.

6th row: P2, yrn, p2, p2tog tbl, p1, p2tog, p2, yrn, *p3, yrn, p2, p2tog tbl, p1, p2tog, p2, yrn; rep from * to last 2 sts, p2.

7th row: K3, yf, k1, k2tog, k1, sl 1, k1, psso, k1, yf, *k5, yf, k1, k2tog, k1, sl 1, k1, psso, k1, yf; rep from * to last 3 sts, k3.

8th row: P4, p2tog tbl, yrn, p1, yrn, p2tog, *p7, p2tog tbl, yrn, p1, yrn, p2tog; rep from * to last 4 sts, p4.

Rep these 8 rows.

Oyster Pattern

Multiple of 6 + 1.

1st row (right side): Knit.

2nd row: P1, *p5 wrapping yarn twice around needle for each st, p1; rep from * to end.

3rd row: K1, *Cluster 5 as follows: pass next 5 sts onto right-hand needle dropping extra loops, pass these 5 sts back onto left-hand needle, [k1, p1, k1, p1, k1] into all 5 sts together wrapping yarn twice around needle for each st, k1; rep from * to end.

4th row: P1, *k5 dropping extra loops, p1; rep from * to end.

5th row: Knit.

6th row: P4, p5 wrapping yarn twice around needle for each st, *p1, p5 wrapping yarn twice around needle for each st; rep from * to last 4 sts, p4.

7th row: K4, Cluster 5 as before, *k1, Cluster 5 as before; rep from * to last 4 sts, k4.

8th row: P4, k5 dropping extra loops, *p1, k5 dropping extra loops; rep from * to last 4 sts, p4.

Rep these 8 rows.

Tulip Lace

Multiple of 8 + 7.

1st row (right side): Knit.

2nd and every alt row: Purl.

3rd row: K3, *yf, sl 1, k1, psso, k6; rep from * to last 4 sts, yf, sl 1, k1, psso, k2.

5th row: K1, *k2tog, yf, k1, yf, sl 1, k1, psso, k3; rep from * to last 6 sts, k2tog, yf, k1, yf, sl 1, k1, psso, k1.

7th row: As 3rd row.

9th row: Knit.

11th row: K7, *yf, sl 1, k1, psso, k6; rep from * to end.

13th row: K5, *k2tog, yf, k1, yf, sl 1, k1, psso, k3; rep from * to last 2 sts, k2.

15th row: As 11th row.

16th row: Purl.

Rep these 16 rows.

Ascending Arrow Panel

Worked over 13 sts on a background of reverse St st.

1st row (right side): P2, yon, sl 1, k1, psso, k5, k2tog, yfrn, p2.

2nd and every alt row: K2, p9, k2.

3rd row: P2, k1, yf, sl 1, k1, psso, k3, k2tog, yf, k1, p2.

5th row: P2, k2, yf, sl 1, k1, psso, k1, k2tog, yf, k2, p2.

7th row: P2, k3, yf, sl 1, k2tog, psso, yf, k3, p2.

8th row: K2, p9, k2.

Rep these 8 rows.

Block your lace knitting for the best visual effect.

Obstacles

Multiple of 14 + 1.

1st row (right side): P2, k2tog, k3, yf, k1, yf, k3, sl 1, k1, psso, *p3, k2tog, k3, yf, k1, yf, k3, sl 1, k1, psso; rep from * to last 2 sts, p2.

2nd, 4th, 6th and 8th rows: K2, p11, *k3, p11; rep from * to last 2 sts, k2.

3rd row: P2, k2tog, k2, yf, k3, yf, k2, sl 1, k1, psso, *p3, k2tog, k2, yf, k3, yf, k2, sl 1, k1, psso; rep from * to last 2 sts, p2.

5th row: P2, k2tog, k1, yf, k5, yf, k1, sl 1, k1, psso, *p3, k2tog, k1, yf, k5, yf, k1, sl 1, k1, psso; rep from * to last 2 sts, p2.

7th row: P2, k2tog, yf, k7, yf, sl 1, k1, psso, *p3, k2tog, yf, k7, yf, sl 1, k1, psso; rep from * to last 2 sts, p2.

9th row: K1, *yf, k3, sl 1, k1, psso, p3, k2tog, k3, yf, k1; rep from * to end.

10th, 12th and 14th rows: P6, k3, *p11, k3; rep from * to last 6 sts, p6.

11th row: K2, yf, k2, sl 1, k1, psso, p3, k2tog, k2, *yf, k3, yf, k2, sl 1, k1, psso, p3, k2tog, k2; rep from * to last 2 sts, yf, k2.

13th row: K3, yf, k1, sl 1, k1, psso, p3, k2tog, k1, *yf, k5, yf, k1, sl 1, k1, psso, p3, k2tog, k1; rep from * to last 3 sts, yf, k3.

15th row: K4, yf, sl 1, k1, psso, p3, k2tog, *yf, k7, yf, sl 1, k1, psso, p3, k2tog; rep from * to last 4 sts, yf, k4.

16th row: P6, k3, *p11, k3; rep from * to last 6 sts, p6.
Rep these 16 rows.

Ostrich Plume Panel

Worked over 13 sts on a background of reverse St st.

1st row (right side): Knit.

2nd row: Purl.

3rd row: K4tog, [yf, k1] 5 times, yf, k4tog.

4th row: Purl.

Rep these 4 rows.

Snowdrop Lace

Multiple of 8 + 5.

1st row (right side): K1, *yf, sl 1 purlwise, k2tog, psso, yf, k5; rep from * to last 4 sts, yf, sl 1 purlwise, k2tog, psso, yf, k1.

2nd and every alt row: Purl.

3rd row: As 1st row.

5th row: K4, *yf, sl 1 purlwise, k1, psso, k1, k2tog, yf, k3; rep from * to last st, k1.

7th row: K1, *yf, sl 1 purlwise, k2tog, psso, yf, k1; rep from * to end.

8th row: Purl.

Rep these 8 rows.

Vertical Arrow Panel

Worked over 13 sts on a background of St st.

1st row (right side): K1, yf, k4, sl 2tog, k1, p2sso, k4, yf, k1.

2nd and every alt row: Purl.

3rd row: K2, yf, k3, sl 2tog, k1, p2sso, k3, yf, k2.

5th row: K3, yf, k2, sl 2tog, k1, p2sso, k2, yf, k3.

7th row: K4, yf, k1, sl 2tog, k1, p2sso, k1, yf, k4.

9th row: K5, yf, sl 2tog, k1, p2sso, yf, k5.

10th row: Purl.

Rep these 10 rows.

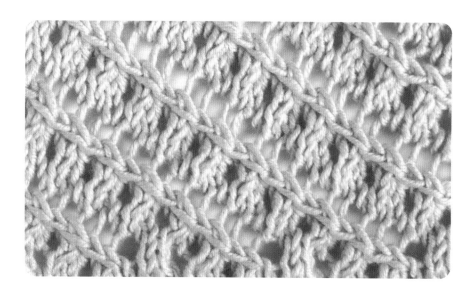

Diagonal Lace

Multiple of 8 + 4.

1st row (right side): K2, *yf, sl 1, k1, psso, k1, k2tog, yf, k3; rep from * to last 2 sts, k2.

2nd row: P7, *p2tog tbl, yrn, p6; rep from * to last 5 sts, p2tog tbl, yrn, p3.

3rd row: K4, *yf, sl 1, k1, psso, k1, k2tog, yf, k3; rep from * to end.

4th row: P5, *p2tog tbl, yrn, p6; rep from * to last 7 sts, p2tog tbl, yrn, p5.

5th row: K1, *k2tog, yf, k3, yf, sl 1, k1, psso, k1; rep from * to last 3 sts, k2tog, yf, k1.

6th row: P3, *p2tog tbl, yrn, p6; rep from * to last st, p1.

7th row: K3, *k2tog, yf, k3, yf, sl 1, k1, psso, k1; rep from * to last st, k1.

8th row: P1, *p2tog tbl, yrn, p6; rep from * to last 3 sts, p2tog tbl, yrn, p1.

Rep these 8 rows.

Lattice Twist with Eyelets

Multiple of 8 + 3.

1st row (right side): K3, *k2tog, yf, k1, yf, sl 1, k1, psso, k3; rep from * to end.

2nd and every alt row: Purl.

3rd row: K2, C2F, k3, C2B, *k1, C2F, k3, C2B; rep from * to last 2 sts, k2.

5th row: K1, C2F, k5, *C3R, k5; rep from * to last 3 sts, C2B, k1.

7th row: K2, yf, sl 1, k1, psso, k3, k2tog, yf, *k1, yf, sl 1, k1, psso, k3, k2tog, yf; rep from * to last 2 sts, k2.

9th row: K3, *C2B, k1, C2F, k3; rep from * to end.

11th row: K4, C3R, *k5, C3R; rep from * to last 4 sts, k4.

12th row: Purl.

Rep these 12 rows.

Chevron Rib

Multiple of 7 + 2.

1st row (right side): K2, *k2tog, yf, k1, yf, sl 1, k1, psso, k2; rep from * to end.

2nd row: Purl.

3rd row: K1, *k2tog, yf, k3, yf, sl 1, k1, psso; rep from * to last st, k1.

4th row: Purl.

Rep these 4 rows.

Filigree Lace

Multiple of 16 + 2.

1st Foundation row (right side): K6, k2tog, yf, k2, yf, sl 1, k1, psso, *k10, k2tog, yf, k2, yf, sl 1, k1, psso; rep from * to last 6 sts, k6.

2nd Foundation row: P5, p2tog tbl, yrn, p4, yrn, p2tog, *p8, p2tog tbl, yrn, p4, yrn, p2tog; rep from * to last 5 sts, p5.

3rd Foundation row: K4, k2tog, yf, k6, yf, sl 1, k1, psso, *k6, k2tog, yf, k6, yf, sl 1, k1, psso; rep from * to last 4 sts, k4.

4th Foundation row: P3, p2tog tbl, yrn, p4, yrn, p2tog, p2, yrn, p2tog, *p4, p2tog tbl, yrn, p4, yrn, p2tog, p2, yrn, p2tog; rep from * to last 3 sts, p3.

1st row: K2, *k2tog, yf, k5, yf, sl 1, k1, psso, k3, yf, sl 1, k1, psso, k2; rep from * to end.

2nd row: P1, *p2tog tbl, yrn, p6, yrn, p2tog, p4, yrn, p2tog; rep from * to last st, p1.

3rd row: K1, sl 1 purlwise, k1, yf, sl 1, k1, psso, k4, yf, sl 1, k1, psso, k2, k2tog, yf, k1, *[sl 1 purlwise] twice, k1, yf, sl 1, k1, psso, k4, yf, sl 1, k1, psso, k2, k2tog, yf, k1; rep from * to last 2 sts, sl 1 purlwise, k1.

4th row: P4, yrn, p2tog, p3, yrn, p2tog, p1, p2tog tbl, *yrn, p6, yrn, p2tog, p3, yrn, p2tog, p1, p2tog tbl; rep from * to last 4 sts, yrn, p4.

5th row: K1, yf, sl 1, k1, psso, k2, yf, sl 1, k1, psso, k4, k2tog, *yf, k4, yf, sl 1, k1, psso, k2, yf, sl 1, k1, psso, k4, k2tog; rep from * to last 5 sts, yf, k5.

6th row: P1, yrn, p2tog, p3, yrn, p2tog, p2, p2tog tbl, *yrn, p5, yrn, p2tog, p3, yrn, p2tog, p2, p2tog tbl; rep from * to last 6 sts, yrn, p6.

7th row: K1, yf, sl 1, k1, psso, k4, yf, sl 1, k1, psso, k2tog, *yf, k6, yf, sl 1, k1, psso, k4, yf, sl 1, k1, psso, k2tog; rep from * to last 7 sts, yf, k7.

8th row: P1, yrn, p2tog, p2, p2tog tbl, yrn, p1, [sl 1 purlwise] twice, p1, yrn, p2tog, *p4, yrn, p2tog, p2, p2tog tbl, yrn, p1, [sl 1 purlwise] twice, p1, yrn, p2tog; rep from * to last 5 sts, p5.

9th row: K1, yf, sl 1, k1, psso, k1, k2tog, yf, k2, C2R, k2, yf, sl 1, k1, psso, *k3, yf, sl 1, k1, psso, k1, k2tog, yf, k2, C2R, k2, yf, sl 1, k1, psso; rep from * to last 4 sts, k4.

10th row: P3, p2tog tbl, yrn, p4, yrn, p2tog, p2, yrn, p2tog, *p4, p2tog tbl, yrn, p4, yrn, p2tog, p2, yrn, p2tog; rep from * to last 3 sts, p3.

Rep the last 10 rows.

Twig and Leaf Insertion

Worked over 13 sts on a background of St st.

1st and every alt row (wrong side): Purl.

2nd row: [K1, yf] twice, sl 1, k2tog, psso, k3, k3tog, [yf, k1] twice.

4th row: K1, yf, k3, yf, sl 1, k1, psso, k1, k2tog, yf, k3, yf, k1. (15 sts)

6th row: K1, yf, sl 1, k1, psso, k1, k2tog, yf, sl 1, k2tog, psso, yf, sl 1, k1, psso, k1, k2tog, yf, k1. (13 sts)

8th row: K1, [yf, sl 1, k1, psso, k1, k2tog, yf, k1] twice.

10th row: As 8th row.

Rep these 10 rows.

Zigzag Openwork

Multiple of 2 + 1.

Note: Sts should only be counted after the 2nd or 4th rows.

1st row (right side): K1, *k2tog; rep from * to end.

2nd row: K1, *M1, k1; rep from * to end.

3rd row: *K2tog; rep from * to last st, k1.

4th row: As 2nd row.

Rep these 4 rows.

Oriel Lace

Multiple of 12 + 1.

1st row (right side): P1, *yb, sl 1, k1, psso, k3, yfrn, p1, yon, k3, k2tog, p1; rep from * to end.

2nd row: K1, *p5, k1; rep from * to end.

Rep the last 2 rows twice more.

7th row: P1, *yon, k3, k2tog, p1, yb, sl 1, k1, psso, k3, yfrn, p1; rep from * to end.

8th row: As 2nd row.

9th row: P2, yon, k2, k2tog, p1, yb, sl 1, k1, psso, k2, *yfrn, p3, yon, k2, k2tog, p1, yb, sl 1, k1, psso, k2; rep from * to last 2 sts, yfrn, p2.

10th row: K2, p4, k1, p4, *k3, p4, k1, p4; rep from * to last 2 sts, k2.

11th row: P3, yon, k1, k2tog, p1, yb, sl 1, k1, psso, k1, *yfrn, p5, yon, k1, k2tog, p1, yb, sl 1, k1, psso, k1; rep from * to last 3 sts, yfrn, p3.

12th row: K3, p3, k1, p3, *k5, p3, k1, p3; rep from * to last 3 sts, k3.

13th row: P4, yon, k2tog, p1, yb, sl 1, k1, psso, *yfrn, p7, yon, k2tog, p1, yb, sl 1, k1, psso; rep from * to last 4 sts, yfrn, p4.

14th row: K4, p2, k1, p2, *k7, p2, k1, p2; rep from * to last 4 sts, k4.

15th row: As 7th row.

16th row: As 2nd row.

Rep the last 2 rows twice more.

21st row: P1, *yb, sl 1, k1, psso, k3, yfrn, p1, yon, k3, k2tog, p1; rep from * to end.

22nd row: As 2nd row.

23rd row: P1, *yb, sl 1, k1, psso, k2, yfrn, p3, yon, k2, k2tog, p1; rep from * to end.

24th row: K1, *p4, k3, p4, k1; rep from * to end.

25th row: P1, *yb, sl 1, k1, psso, k1, yfrn, p5, yon, k1, k2tog, p1; rep from * to end.

26th row: K1, *p3, k5, p3, k1; rep from * to end.

27th row: P1, *yb, sl 1, k1, psso, yfrn, p7, yon, k2tog, p1; rep from * to end.

28th row: K1, *p2, k7, p2, k1; rep from * to end.

Rep these 28 rows.

Diamond Panel

Worked over 11 sts on a background of St st.

1st row (right side): P2, k2tog, [k1, yf] twice, k1, sl 1, k1, psso, p2.

2nd and every alt row: K2, p7, k2.

3rd row: P2, k2tog, yf, k3, yf, sl 1, k1, psso, p2.

5th row: P2, k1, yf, sl 1, k1, psso, k1, k2tog, yf, k1, p2.

7th row: P2, k2, yf, sl 1, k2tog, psso, yf, k2, p2.

8th row: As 2nd row.

Rep these 8 rows.

Gardinia Lace Panel

Worked over 12 sts on a background of St st.

Note: Sts should not be counted after 1st row.

1st row (right side): K3, [k2tog, yf] twice. sl 1, k1, psso, k3.

2nd row: P2, p2tog tbl, yrn, p1, inc 1 in next st, p1, yrn, p2tog, p2.

3rd row: K1, k2tog, yf, k6, yf, sl 1, k1, psso, k1.

4th row: P2tog tbl, yrn, p8, yrn, p2tog.

5th row: K1, yf, k3, k2tog, sl 1, k1, psso, k3, yf, k1.

6th row: P2, yrn, p2, p2tog tbl, p2tog, p2, yrn, p2.

7th row: K3, yf, k1, k2tog, sl 1, k1, psso, k1, yf, k3.

8th row: P4, yrn, p2tog tbl, p2tog, yrn, p4.

Rep these 8 rows.

Hourglass Eyelets

Multiple of 6 + 1.

1st row (right side): K6, *p1, k5; rep from * to last st, k1.

2nd row: K1, *p5, k1; rep from * to end.

3rd row: K1, *yf, sl 1, k1, psso, p1, k2tog, yf, k1; rep from * to end.

4th row: K1, p2, *k1, p5; rep from * to last 4 sts, k1, p2, k1.

5th row: K3, *p1, k5; rep from * to last 4 sts, p1, k3.

6th row: As 4th row.

7th row: K1, *k2tog, yf, k1, yf, sl 1, k1, psso, p1; rep from * to last 6 sts, k2tog, yf, k1, yf, sl 1, k1, psso, k1.

8th row: As 2nd row.

Rep these 8 rows.

Branch Panel

Worked over 12 sts on a background of reverse St st.

1st row (right side): K2tog, k5, yf, k1, yf, k2, sl 1, k1, psso.

2nd and every alt row: Purl.

3rd row: K2tog, k4, yf, k3, yf, k1, sl 1, k1, psso.

5th row: K2tog, k3, yf, k5, yf, sl 1, k1, psso.

7th row: K2tog, k2, yf, k1, yf, k5, sl 1, k1, psso.

9th row: K2tog, k1, yf, k3, yf, k4, sl 1, k1, psso.

11th row: K2tog, yf, k5, yf, k3, sl 1, k1, psso.

12th row: Purl.

Rep these 12 rows.

Lacy Rib

Multiple of 3 + 1.

1st row (right side): K1, *k2tog, yfrn, p1; rep from * to last 3 sts, k2tog, yf, k1.

2nd row: P3, *k1, p2; rep from * to last 4 sts, k1, p3.

3rd row: K1, yf, sl 1, k1, psso, *p1, sl 1, yon, k1, psso; rep from * to last st, k1.

4th row: As 2nd row.

Rep these 4 rows.

abbreviations

[ ]	work instructions within brackets as many times as directed
( )	work instructions within parentheses in the place directed
*	repeat instructions following the single asterisk as directed
* *	repeat instructions following the asterisks as directed
alt	alternate
C2B	cable 2 back
C2F	cable 2 front
C3R	cable 3 right – slip next 2 sts onto cable needle and hold at back of work, knit next st from left-hand needle, then knit sts from cable needle.
C4B	cable-back 4 back – slip next 2 sts onto cable needle and hold at back of work, knit next 2 sts from left-hand needle, then knit sts from cable needle.
C4F	cable 4 front – slip next 2 sts onto cable needle and hold at front of work, knit next 2 sts from left-hand needle, then knit sts from cable needle.
C6F	cable 6 front – slip next 3 sts onto cable needle and hold at front of work, knit next 3 sts from left-hand needle, then knit sts from cable needle.
inc	increase(s)
k	knit
k2tog	knit 2 together
K5W	knit next 5 stitches wrapping yarn twice around needle for each stitch
KB1	knit into back of next stitch
KW2	knit next stitch wrapping yarn twice around needle
LH	left hand
M1	make 1
MB	make bobble
p	purl
p2tog	purl 2 together
PB1	purl into back of next stitch
psso	pass slip stitch over
rep	repeat(s)

RH	right side
sl	slip
st(s)	stitch(es)
St st	stocking stitch
T3F	Twist 3 flip – slip next 2 sts onto cable needle and hold at front of work, purl next st from left-hand needle, then knit sts from cable needle.
T3B	Twist 3 back – slip next st onto cable needle and hold at back of work, knit next 2 sts from left-hand needle, then purl st from cable needle.
tbl	through back loop
tog	together
WS	wrong side
yb	yarn to the back
yf	yarn to the front
yfon	yarn forward and over needle
yfrn	with yarn in front
yo/yon	yarn over needle
yrn	yarn around needle

index

resources

Rowan
Green Lane Mill
Holmfirth
HD9 2DX
England

Other titles currently available in the Harmony Guides series: